Tommy Atkins' War Stories

Tommy Atkins'
War Stories

Fourteen First Hand Accounts from
the Ranks of the British Army
During Queen Victoria's Empire

LEONAUR

Tommy Atkins' War Stories: Fourteen First Hand Accounts from the Ranks of the British Army During Queen Victoria's Empire

This book was first published in 1897 under the title *Told from the Ranks*, collected by E. Milton Small.

Published by Leonaur Ltd

Material original to this edition
copyright © 2005 Leonaur Ltd

ISBN (10 digit): 1-84677-037-8 (hardcover)
ISBN (13 digit): 978-1-84677-037-1 (hardcover)

ISBN (10 digit): 1-84677-022-X (softcover)
ISBN (13 digit): 978-1-84677-022-7 (softcover)

http://www.leonaur.com

Publisher's Notes

Contents

Who Was Tommy Atkins?	9
Preface	11
Recollections of the Indian Mutiny	13
With the 49th in the Crimea	25
With the Guards in Egypt	41
The Charge of the Six Hundred	57
With Wolseley in Ashanti	71
Alma, Inkermann and Magdala	81
With the Gunners at Tel-el-Kebir	91
Russian Guns and Indian Rebels	101
Rough Work in the Crimea	123
In the Maori Rising	141
Facing the Zulus	151
From Sebastopol to Lucknow	167
Sent to Save Gordon	181
On the March to Chitral	193

Appendix

Tommy by Rudyard Kipling	**205**

Who Was Tommy Atkins?

Tommy Atkins is the familiar nick-name used to describe ordinary soldiers serving in the British Army. Today, it is more usually abbreviated to tommy or tommies.

The term dates back as far as the 1740s, when it is known to have been used in correspondence, but the official origin given is that Tommy Atkins was first used in 1815 as a generic name on War Office forms. The name came into wider useage during the Boer War in the later nineteenth century.

When Rudyard Kipling's poem, Tommy, was published in his book Barrack Room Ballads in 1892 it entered the vocabularies of ordinary people where it has remained in use ever since.

According to folklore Wellington himself chose the name for the War Office form, inspired by memories of a dying soldier he met during the Battle of Boxtel in 1794. The man had a sabre wound on his head, a bayonet wound in his chest and a bullet wound in his lungs.

The man's name was Tommy Atkins, and his last words to Wellington were:

"It's alright sir. It's all in a day's work."

Preface

The following "yarns" consist of reminiscences communicated by privates and non-commissioned officers belonging, or formerly belonging, to the British army. They make no pretension to being polished, carefully-worded narratives; they simply give, in a plain, rough-and-ready way, the story of the various campaigns in which the narrators personally took part. They are not so much history as "footnotes to history." Many of the incidents described are relatively of no importance, but they nevertheless bring home forcibly to the reader the trying or perilous nature of the work done by the common soldier.

It is gratifying to our pride as a nation to find that the patient endurance and self-forgetting heroism which were displayed "on Alma's heights," and in the snowy trenches before Sebastopol, have had their counterpart, again and again, in those many "little wars" which have been undertaken in our own day for the safe-guarding or the extension of the Empire.

Tommy Atkins' War Stories: 1

Recollections of the Indian Mutiny

By Gunner MacCallam

Royal Artillery

Gunner MacCallam was present at the
outbreak of the Indian Mutiny at
Meerut and here describes
the actions thereafter.

Recollections
of the Indian Mutiny

I enlisted in 1852, in the Royal Artillery, then stationed at
Woolwich, and six months afterwards went out to India, where,
after spending some few years at various stations, I found myself
in 1857 at Meerut, with a regiment of infantry, one of dragoons,
and a troop and battery of artillery, numbering altogether one
thousand seven hundred and seventeen men, under the command of Major-General Hewitt.

There were also two regiments of native infantry and one
of light cavalry, numbering in all two thousand seven hundred,
and these men, with others, had been pretty mutinous. I remember, on the 6th of May, cartridges, made especially for the
purpose of satisfying their religious scruples, were offered to the
native cavalry, but eighty-five troopers refused to accept them,
and they were tried by court-martial, and sentenced to various
terms of imprisonment extending from five to ten years. On
the 9th they were put in irons, and conducted to prison under
a guard of Sepoys. We were posted at a distance of three miles
from the native camp.

On the following day, which was Sunday, at about five o'clock
in the afternoon, the native regiments rose in mutiny, fired on their
officers, rushed to the prison, rescued the mutineers and upwards of
a thousand convicts confined there, and set the building on fire.

English people were killed wherever they could be found. Bun-
galows were blazing in all directions, and the streets were filled with
crowds of murderers, rushing into the English residences, and carrying off all the valuables they could lay their hands on.

In our distant barracks we were preparing for church parade, but, as soon as the alarm reached us, we started off in haste, and, coming upon the rascals at their work of destruction, we poured into them volleys of grape and musketry, drove them from the town and pursued them in their retreat, killing great numbers. Many of them escaped to Delhi, thirty-five miles off, where three regiments of native infantry and a battery of native artillery were stationed, under Brigadier-General Graves, without a single company of British soldiers. They crowded into the city early on the following day, shouting their battle-cry, "Deen, Deen!" and cutting down every European they met, and even exceeding the atrocities of Meerut.

A few of the English officers and residents had taken refuge in the powder magazine, which was in charge of two officers and three or four subalterns, where they made a most gallant defence against the united forces of the rebels, repelling their attacks by volleys of grape. Thousands still pressed forward, applying scaling-ladders to the walls, and, just at the moment of their success, Lieutenant Willoughby, one of the officers in charge, having laid a train to the powder, gave the signal for it to be fired by Conductor Scully, and instantly the building, with hundreds of Sepoys who were crowding into it, was blown into the air.

The handful of defenders managed to escape in the confusion, carrying with them the blackened and almost lifeless body of the gallant Willoughby, who died in Meerut shortly afterwards, and leaving behind the scorched and shattered body of the noble Scully.

A few Englishmen who had attempted to hold a small fortified bastion within the Cashmere gate, called the Mainguard, were massacred by the treacherous Sepoy guard on whom they depended. Others, who had fled to the palace for protection, were murdered in the presence of the King, who was over eighty years old, his sons being also present, and thus every British resident in Delhi was slaughtered.

It is very evident that the rebels intended to clear their country of its conquerors, for I learned that when a native servant was anxious to spare a child or hide an Englishwoman, the mutineers repeated the following Persian verse:—

"To extinguish the fire and leave a spark,
To kill a snake and preserve its young,
Is not the wisdom of men of sense."

On returning to Meerut after chasing the mutineers, we were all ordered to remove to Dum-Dum, which is a large piece of ground enclosed by a wall, as far as I can remember about eight feet high, against which we threw up intrenchrnents and earthworks, and made loopholes for the rifles and embrasures for the guns. There were three large buildings within the enclosure, used as laboratories, and into these we put about a hundred and fifty women and children, and when all arrangements were completed the troops moved off to Delhi, leaving me with some two hundred men of all regiments, some sick and some convalescent, to mount guard; and here we remained for some months, taking turns in watching night and day, with no letters, no papers, no tobacco, and no news from outside. When the country round us was quieted down a little, some fifty or sixty of us were relieved, and, marching to Umballah, we joined a flying column, and pushed on to join the Central India Field Force at Jubbulpore, under Sir George Whitlock. Thence we made for Saugor, where the right wing of the 42nd Native Infantry had mutinied while the left wing had remained loyal, and the two wings had fought a regular pitched battle on the parade ground before we arrived, but hearing that we were only a few miles off, the right wing beat an orderly retreat towards Delhi, marching away with their colours flying.

As a precautionary measure we took the arms from the loyal

left wing, but allowed them to carry their ramrods, and they marched with us through the jungle. On nearing Loghasi our advance guard came upon a large body of the enemy on a prominent hill, the sides of which were covered with dense jungle.

We did good work with our guns, and our infantry had a hard fight for the hill. After a severe struggle, in which we lost a good many men, we succeeded in driving the rebels from their position, capturing their guns, and taking one hundred and forty prisoners. The next day every one of them was hung on the trees surrounding the camp, simply hauled off the ground by ropes around their necks, and left to die and be devoured by the birds.

We pressed on again for a considerable distance, and encamped; and about eight o'clock in the evening we marched out, leaving the camp standing. We took up a position with the artillery on each flank, infantry in the centre, cavalry in the rear, and cavalry vedettes to cover the front. As night fell we threw out outlying pickets, and so remained until four the next morning, when, without sound of bugle or beat of drum, we advanced, and after proceeding about three miles, the enemy's guns opened the ball, to which we quickly replied, and soon the fighting became general.

We advanced, driving the enemy across a river, which was a shallow tributary of the Ganges, I believe. Crossing the river with an advance guard, we found, to our great surprise, that the mutineers had dug rifle-pits on a level with the river banks, which extended for more than half a mile, and from these they potted our men off, one at a time, as we waded across.

I incautiously peeped into one of these pits, and my curiosity nearly cost me my life, for inside were three Pandies, or Sepoys, who immediately opened fire on me and a chum who was just behind me. We retired a few yards, but came back and despatched the three of them with our carbines, taking their rifles, belts, and ammunition into the camp as trophies. Their commissariat supply consisted of a chatty of water, a few small bags of rice, and one or two chupatties, or native cakes.

When the column had gained the opposite bank, the infantry deployed into line, and captured a large village on our left, where they slaughtered large numbers of the rebels, all wearing Her Majesty's uniform. There were no prisoners taken, and no quarter given.

A rather strange incident occurred here. A black troop of horse artillery was ordered to the front, covered by the 12th Lancers; when in a swinging trot, without a word of command, they broke into a rapid gallop and endeavoured to join the rebels. The lead driver of No. 1 gun was immediately shot by the English officer in charge, and this checked the remainder, who were ordered to the rear, while the English troop of horse artillery, dashing to the front, came into action with a most destructive fire, being covered by the 12th Lancers. The mutineer cavalry made a move to outflank our batteries, but were checked by a most brilliant charge of the 12th Lancers, in which Sir George Wombwell's horse was shot under him.

The mutineers stood their ground well for about fifteen minutes, and then broke, and retired in the utmost confusion. It was a glorious sight to see them run. We limbered up and followed them for a considerable distance, firing at them as long as they remained in masses, until at last they became scattered in small groups all over the plain, whilst their cavalry escaped across the river, upon the banks of which, I remember, there was a large fort, which our siege-train opened fire on and knocked to pieces. We advanced up the banks of the river, and encamped for the night on the ground lately occupied by the mutineers.

We then had to bury our dead before turning in; we had two chaplains with us, one a Protestant and the other a Catholic, and they read the services over the graves which held our men. The blacks, of whom I should say there were a thousand dead on the field, were left for the jackals and vultures, which do all the scavenging in India.

Early in the morning we struck camp, and after a sharp encounter took possession of the city of Banda, and soon had the British flag once more flying over the palace, while the troops were paraded, and a royal salute fired, after which some of us were quartered in the palace.

This was the first engagement of the 3rd Madras European Regiment, now the 108th, which was raised at Bellary in November 1854 by Sir George Whitlock, and called by him his "younkers." The dash and gallantry of this young regiment could not be surpassed, and brought cheers from the old soldiers who watched their movements.

Sir George was delighted with them, and after the fight paraded them and praised them loudly. He was a most excellent officer, and a great favourite with the men. He rode a mule in the action before Banda, and it was a common sight, when on the march, to see him allow the drummer boys to ride in turns upon it while he walked by its side, for he took a fatherly interest in the young boys of the regiment.

For nearly the whole of the month following, the General and Commissioner were trying the mutineers, so that every morning before breakfast the infantry had to take part in the execution of between twenty and thirty of them, whom they hung on a large gallows in front of the palace gates. The artillery and cavalry had always enough to do to look after their horses.

The Rajah of the city got away, but we managed to capture his Prime Minister, and after standing his trial he was brought out for execution. I was close to him, and saw what a fine big fellow he was, weighing over twenty-two stone, and wearing a dress covered with gold and jewels. He was offered his liberty if he would disclose where the Rajah was hiding. He called out,

"You English dog!" and spat at the officer who had charge of him, whereupon he was hoisted off his feet, and hung there writhing and kicking for ever so long.

I believe the sergeant who had charge of the hanging party obtained possession of the diamond from his turban, and the other jewels, I suppose, were not left for the birds. But we had nothing like the loot that one would expect, seeing the vast riches that were strewn about. We were unable to carry much about with us, and in consequence had to leave it for the natives who were under the command of the prize agents. Many kind promises were made by the generals, so that we all expected to live in plenty to the end of our days.

On the 8th of June 1858, we marched from Banda, for the capture of Kirwee and all its gold bricks, of which we had heard so much. We arrived at the banks of the river on the 10th, when the Rajah, Naran Roe, accompanied by his two sons and a large retinue of servants, came out and gave up his sword to our General, after which he was placed a prisoner under a European guard, and the palace was garrisoned by two companies of the 42nd Light Infantry.

The three hundred wives of the Rajah, on our approach, fled from the palace, snatching up what treasures they could find, and not stopping to pick up the valuables they dropped in their flight. We found the place strewn with an indescribable assortment of trinkets, jewels, slippers, bracelets, chains, and female finery, and on resuming our march we came upon fifty of these women hiding in a small village.

One of the Rajah's sons had shot his English tutor a day or so before we arrived. I had several talks with him while we were in charge of the palace, and found him an interesting and intelligent young man. Eventually he and his father and brother were sent to the Andaman Islands.

Most of the native troops, on our arrival marched out of the city at the opposite side, and took up a position on a high hill, posting themselves behind a breastwork of large bales of cotton, each about nine feet long.

About three in the morning we started to attack their position, and got under the hill before they were aware of our approach. We went up in three divisions, each division having two mortars, while the cavalry and artillery went round to the right to cut off their retreat. The infantry swarmed up the hill, and found the rebels preparing their breakfast. A fierce struggle ensued, and we, with the guns, had our hands full to load and fire, mowing down the men as they endeavoured to fly. The slaughter was tremendous. We took, I should say, three hundred prisoners, and then came that horrible butchery which Englishmen practised then for the first and last time -- and then, I suppose, only as a necessity; for the mutiny had to be stamped out, and I am sure we all expected to lose our lives in trying to regain possession of the country.

Our prisoners had no fear of death, and were marvellous in their immovability. We took them out into an open space and tied them together six at a time, placing them with their backs turned towards half a dozen guns, and at a little distance from them.

As we placed them in position they never moved a muscle, and some of them spat at us and called us dogs. When the word was given to fire, thirty-six of them were blown to pieces. This was repeated over and over again, and as the heaps accumulated, we drew the guns back, and continued the slaughter till the men were all destroyed.

The value of the riches found in Kirwee was beyond the power of man to imagine. Heaps of jewels and gold were found stowed away, and the gold bricks were so numerous that it took thirty bullock-waggons to remove the treasure, an Englishman and a Sepoy being placed to guard each waggon.

At a parade about this time the General said that every man who heard him, if he were spared to return to England, would be worth £500. Alas! the most fortunate of us only received £75, and that after a considerable delay, owing to a lawsuit brought by General Rose, who was in command of another column a hundred miles away, and who claimed to be entitled to half the Kirwee prize-money.

I know several old soldiers who have to keep themselves and their wives on seven shillings a week, while I have heard it said that the Government has still half a million of prize-money un-distributed. I suppose I must not complain, for I am not hard pinched, although I imagine I could stand the trial of a few extra shillings a week to add to my comforts, while sitting by my own fireside, and looking back upon my twenty-one years of service.

Tommy Atkins' War Stories: 2

With the 49th in the Crimea

By Edward Hyde

49th Regiment

Edward Hyde served with the
49th (Princess Charlotte of Wales
Hertfordshire) Regiment at the
crossing of the Alma, Inkermann
& the attack on the Redan.

With the 49th
in the Crimea

On the 20th of November 1841, I joined the 49th (Princess Charlotte of Wales' Hertfordshire) Regiment, now linked with the 66th (Berkshire) Regiment.

In 1850, or '51, six companies of the regiment went to Corfu in the Ionian Islands, and I was left in Ireland with four companies to form the depot.

At the end of two years our regiment embarked for Malta, where I joined them, and there we remained until orders were received to proceed to Scutari, opposite Constantinople, in preparation for the Crimean War. Here we saw many wounded Turks brought to hospital from the war, which was then in progress between them and the Russians. As soon as the sun sets at Scutari the darkness comes on rapidly, and as there is, therefore, no twilight, the nights seemed very long. However, we were always up for early morning drill about four, sometimes even before daybreak.

We left here for Varrna, and, having landed, we marched inland for about sixteen miles, and pitched our camp, but were soon attacked with cholera. The 30th Regiment suffered terribly, losing as many as twenty men a day, but in our regiment we only had nine cases. We shifted our ground farther up the country by the doctor's orders.

At length we marched to Varna and embarked for the Crimea, landing at Old Fort, Eupatoria, on the 14th September. The scene was a very lively one, on account of the large number of ships and troops. We disembarked at once in flat-bottomed boats, which, I believe, belonged to the Turks. The weather was mild and fine, but at night we had rain till morning. The troops were formed into four divisions, of which mine was the second. As we marched along, three men of my company fell out of the ranks, and we never saw them again, and could not find out what became of them.

When we approached the Alma (river), we found the Russians had set fire to some stacks to windward of us, and the smoke nearly blinded us. Here we had to form fours and get through a narrow break in the underwood, then open out again and rush across the river, with the water in some places up to our waists. The nearer we got to the Russians the less danger we were in, on account of their not being able to sight, their guns upon us quickly.

We went up the hills without much difficulty, helping ourselves up with the brushwood and branches of trees that grew on some parts of the heights where we were. We lost a good many men, the troops in the middle getting the worst of it. The Fusiliers and Guards suffered greatly. My division was next to the French, and some of us went up shoulder to shoulder, while the ships at the mouth of the river fired shot and shell over our heads upon the Russians on the heights above us.

Amongst the many wounded in the fight were three brothers, whom I knew intimately; one lost a leg, and another lost both; the third brother escaped at Alma, but met his death later on. The French, as we struggled upward, were continually calling out "Moscow!" and keeping up a rapid fire. The Zouaves, who are fine soldiers, picked from the French infantry regiments, behaved splendidly, and fought like lions. They wore scarlet knee-breeches, brown gaiters, and short blue jackets with yellow braid. The Algerian Zouaves were all blacks, commanded by French officers.

As we neared the top of the heights, the Russian infantry went off at the double towards Sebastopol, and we saw num-

bers of carriages going away with them. Perhaps they contained wounded officers, -- I can't say, -- but some said they were ladies and gentlemen who had come out to witness our destruction, and had been disappointed.

We peppered after them till the bugles sounded "Cease firing"; then we turned our attention to our wounded. This was my first battlefield, and I can't very well describe my feelings; whether it was fear or excitement I don't know, but I seemed dazed, and went wherever the others went, and did whatever they did; there was nothing to be gained by hanging back.

I saw some shocking sights, but we soon became accustomed to the smell of blood and the sight of carnage and butchery that surrounded us, and did the best we could to carry all the wounded to the beach, where the sailors took them on board ship in boats. There were in all about two thousand eight hundred wounded English and French.

The Russians carried little leather pouches, strapped round their right leg below the knee, under the trousers, in which they carried their money, and although it was against orders to touch the contents, many did so, sometimes finding as much as four dollars in a pouch.

After burying the dead, we started towards Sebastopol, our first camp being at Katcha, where we found lots of grapes growing on the ground like peas in a field. The doctors cautioned us against eating them, as they were green, but we could not resist the temptation.

Next night we rested on the banks of the river Belbeck, and the following day we pushed on to Balaklava, which we found deserted, and entered without a shot being fired. All our cavalry were quartered here, and we pretty well filled the harbour with our men-of-war and vessels loaded with stores and provisions.

I remember taking pity upon a cat and three kittens which I found starving in Sebastopol, and these I brought away.

We left Balaklava and pitched our camp at Inkermann, and every day and night men were told off to dig trenches, so that we could approach the Russian batteries of Sebastopol under cover.

Matters went on thus till the 25th October, when the Russians were expected to attack the town of Balaklava. We could see their troops moving forward pretty thickly from where my regiment was stationed; but, although we were under arms all that day and night, we heard no details of the battle till the afternoon, when all was over. We had been waiting, expecting the enemy to attack our position, but they did not do so.

On the following day, about five in the morning, the second division of outlying pickets, about two hundred in number, were driven back into our camp. Lieutenant Conolley, of the 49th, who was in charge of them, had broken his sword in the fight, and continuing the struggle with his telescope, had fallen, shot through the body. He was brought in by some of the men, and, when he recovered sufficiently, was invalided home, and appointed a major of the Grenadier Guards. I saw him four years afterwards at Aldershot, when he called me to him, and asked me if I remembered him, but he had grown so plump that I could hardly recognise him.

As soon as it was light enough, the whole of the second division advanced and attacked the Russians, driving them back with a loss of three hundred, while our loss was about a hundred in killed, wounded, and prisoners.

In our division, which was the right attack, we had to put on our overcoats and accoutrements and buckle up at eight in the evening, and were not allowed to unfasten till five in the morning, and not even then if there were any signs of an attack. Almost every night there were false alarms, and the quarter guard would quietly call to us to stand to our arms, and the men would silently turn out and stand ready. As soon as belts came off in the morning, we were all busy lighting fires, where possible, and getting breakfast. We had no fires during the night except here and there.

In the early morning of the 5th of November, I had been lighting a fire to make some water hot in a three-legged iron pot, which had been brought up from Balaklava. The weather was raw, cold, and terribly foggy, so that we could not see three yards before us. As usual, we stood to arms about half-past five to unbelt and dismiss, when suddenly the bells of Sebastopol began to peal merrily. I should think all the bells they had were ringing, and, before the order was given to dismiss, grape and canister began to fall all around us.

I may explain that, as far as I know, grape is shot weighing about five ounces, fastened into bunches of four or five, with spunyarn or something, which gives way directly they leave the gun. Canister is small shot of different sizes, put into tin canisters, which burst and allow the shot to spread in all directions when fired.

Our picket, having fired in the direction of the advancing enemy, fell back, and we were then ordered to form in brigades and advance up the hill, at the top of which we lay down for about an hour without firing a shot, although the Russian bullets were whizzing over our heads.

Presently came the order to advance again, and the first to fall was our Adjutant, Lieutenant Armstrong, who was shot in the head, and fell from his horse very near where I was standing. Colonel Dalton, who was in command, threw out skirmishers, and I was sent with others to a small ravine, where the Russians were coming up thickly. We were commanded by an officer of artillery, whose name I do not know. There were a lot of large stones lying about, and with them we made a breastwork, and, notwithstanding all the efforts of the Russians, they could not get over our barricade, and had to beat a retreat, and as they went we let them have our bullets in their backs. There were only twenty of us behind the breastwork, but the enemy did not come nearer than ten yards, not knowing how many, were behind us.

My company was sent to take charge of the two-gun battery, where about eighteen or twenty men were firing at the advancing Russians with two eighteen-pounders. This battery was only a simple piece of earthwork thrown up on three sides of a square, with two embrasures in it for the guns. It had been built under fire, and consequently was only a very rough affair.

Soon the Russian infantry got right up to it, and clambered up the front and sides of it, and we had a hard job to keep them out. Directly we saw their heads above the parapet, or looking into the embrasures, we fired at them or bayoneted them as fast as we could. They came on like ants; no sooner was one knocked backwards than another clambered over the dead bodies to take his place, all of them yelling and shouting. We in the battery were not quiet, you may be sure, and what with cheering and shouting, the thud of blows, the clash of bayonets and swords, the ping of the bullets, the whistling of the shells, the foggy atmosphere, and the smell of the powder and blood, the scene inside the battery where we were was beyond the power of man to imagine or describe. We had to fight to save our lives.

In the battle[1] the Russians numbered about fifty thousand men, while the French and English together only mustered something like fourteen thousand. I don't believe the commanding officers could describe the fight, much less a private soldier. The ground was so rough and uneven that the men seemed to break up into parties without commanders, and to fight till all were killed or successful in driving the enemy off. The Russians seemed to outnumber us on all sides.

I remember that where I was, at another part of the day, we

---

1. This was the famous Battle of Inkermann.

were keeping them back well, when some French troops came up behind us, and could not fire for fear of hitting our men. Suddenly their lines opened, and we retired through them, so that, having cleared the ground, the French let out a murderous fire, which completely checked the advance.

Not far from the two-gun battery, the "Grey Battery" of field guns was firing upon the Russians, who were advancing in dense masses, and somehow or other our men got the worst of it, and the enemy's artillery knocked our horses, guns, and carriages to pieces.

The fight continued well into the afternoon, and then the Russians retired, leaving about twelve thousand dead and wounded on the field. Our loss was somewhere about two thousand six hundred men killed and wounded, besides forty-two officers killed and one hundred and three wounded; while the French killed and wounded numbered one thousand seven hundred and twenty-six or thereabouts.

The following day was a sad one, for we were occupied in the mournful duty of digging pits, twenty or thirty feet square, into which we laid the dead as closely as they could be packed; the Russians, as before, leaving their dead and wounded for us to attend to, knowing that we must do so for our own sakes. Yet all the while we were so engaged they kept up a continual fire upon us from their forts, earthworks, and rifle-pits round Sebastopol.

We found the bottles of the enemy contained raw spirit, and from what I saw of the fight I believe many of their men were drunk when they came on the field.

About fifty yards from where I was quartered, the Russian wounded were brought and laid out. They were then taken one at a time to a bench, where our doctors amputated their wounded or shattered limbs. I never went near to watch the operations, as I could see more than enough from where I was, but many of our men had become so callous that they looked on at the dreadful work from sheer curiosity. On the other hand, many had to be there to assist, and others were told off to bury the severed limbs, which was a dreadful task.

We now settled down to spend the winter, which was coming on pretty severely. Unfortunately, a violent hurricane occurred on the 14th, and fifteen transports foundered, with clothing, stores, and baggage on board, including one called The Prince, which had our regiment's clothing and a cargo worth £500,000. The French also lost a lot of vessels; and it was said that more than a thousand lives were lost, besides about £2,000,000 worth of shipping.

Owing to this disaster, we began to feel the want of warm clothing, and our condition became most miserable. I had my boots on for three months without taking them off, until at last they dropped to pieces. No wonder the standing order against plundering the dead was broken. I secured two good pairs of boots which reached almost to my knees. Our doctor saw one pair of them standing outside my tent door, and, as his boots were very much worn, and these were about his size, he admired them very much. I determined to make him a present of them, and took them up to his tent and gave them to his orderly. By and by the orderly brought me down a sovereign in payment.

The only English money we saw was gold -- new sovereigns direct from the Mint. We used to get them changed at a row of shanties which some Maltese, Greeks, and other camp followers had erected near a windmill, and where they sold grocery and other necessaries at fabulous prices, and reaped a rich harvest.

Some time afterwards, when I was in Sebastopol, the right siege-train was blown up near these shanties; I don't know how. It smashed the windmill to pieces, and demolished all the shops, scattering their contents in all directions, and killing many of the traders. I heard that our men who went to bury the dead found a rare lot of sovereigns among the ruins.

The nights spent in the trenches were dismal enough. "We were like moles working our way towards the Russian batteries, and getting nearer and nearer by slow degrees. Not a night passed without casualties, so that when we started at night we could never tell whether we should get back to the camp in the morning. Some nights were worse than others, for the Russians made attacks upon us, and we had hard work to drive them off. I remember finding one of our sergeants with sixteen bayonet wounds on his body. Yet we were always like bull-dogs, and never once lost possession of our trenches.

One night, soon after dusk, a party of my company was ordered to carry fascines down towards Sebastopol, to erect a battery under the direction of an Engineer officer. Off we started, but, after wandering about in the darkness for some time, we lost ourselves, and were ordered to lie down while the officer groped his way about and found the place we wanted. He did not succeed till about midnight, and when he returned we were most of us asleep.

However, we soon set to work with a will, and, having found the desired spot, got the battery built under cover of the darkness. The sailors had dragged up eight Armstrong guns, and these afterwards played upon the Russian shipping, and were the first Armstrongs fired in the Crimea. I naturally took an interest in their work, and was pleased to know they set at least one ship on fire.

I shall never forget one night I spent in the sandbag battery, in which we had two mortars and a few guns which were fired every now and then, but the Russians kept up a continual fire upon that battery during the night, and all we could do was to lie as snugly as we could under cover. It sounded like thousands of musket shots peppering round us, and every now and then a heavy thud told when a shot hit the ground near us. The bags, which held the earth of which the battery was built, were all burnt to pieces, and it was not till about four in the morning, just before daybreak, that the firing slackened. We were relieved at five o'clock, and were glad to hurry back to camp and get a little sleep.

Time passed on, and every day we were at work in the trenches where we could do so without exposing ourselves too much. Most of the work was done after dark, and, as we had no lights, this was rather a difficult job; however, the nights were not always pitch dark, and we could see a little what we were about.

There was a disused stone quarry between us and the town, which the Russians had strongly fortified. One night we made an attack upon it, which had been carefully planned. I believe about one hundred and fifty of our regiment were engaged! The Russians were on the alert, and we kept up a continuous fire of musketry upon them, which they returned, and also sent several eighteen-inch shells amongst us. With a dash our men made for their works, and it was sharp work for all of us for a short time, until the Russians retired and left us in possession, which was another step in the right direction, as we always advanced and never once retired from a trench.

Next day the Russians showed a flag of truce, which was the only one I remember, and both sides sent out parties to collect their dead and wounded. Some of us waved our hands in a friendly way to the Russians, who mingled with us in the work. I was not a little surprised to find among them an Irishman. I believe he had been a sailor, and had married a Russian woman, but we had no time to gossip. He said there were two or three more in their ranks, but he declined to come back with us.

The truce lasted about three hours, and, having brought in the wounded, we looked about to find a soft place in which to dig a pit, and there we buried our dead. We had no time for sentiment, and had become a hardened lot, as rough as gold-diggers, and much less cleanly. Our uncut hair and beards gave us a fierce appearance, added to which our clothes were ragged, and many of us had to bind bits of sacking round our legs for warmth.

The day after the fight at the quarries I wanted to make some coffee for some of my companions and myself, and I went into a trench to light a fire, so as to be sheltered from the Russian shells. I found some Rifles busy round a fire, and they kindly allowed me to boil my water, but while I was waiting for it, a shot hit the parapet of the trench and sent a large stone bang on my chest. I was knocked down insensible, and when I came to, I found them standing round me thinking I was wounded; I thought so too, but was glad to find nothing much the matter except a bruise about the size of my hand. So I took my hot water and went back to my companions, who were beginning to wonder what had become of me.

After spending nine weary months in this prolonged siege, our troops made an attack early in the morning of the 18th June on the enemy's principal fortification, the Redan, an earthwork constructed, with the aid of timber, to accommodate three or four thousand men, as far as I could judge when I got inside it afterwards.

They had masked the guns to make the place look weak, and when we made the grand rush we were swept down like grass before the scythe. Our officers fell fast, and when it was found impossible to get over the abattis, the bugle sounded "Retire"; many of us, in the confusion, did not hear the call, and there we were struggling to take possession of the place, which we then found impregnable. Under a concentrated fire from all sides we had to retire, leaving heaps of dead behind us, and this on the anniversary of Waterloo!

My regiment, before the fight, numbered about five hundred men, but, when the roll was called in the evening, we found nearly two hundred missing.

Our senior Captain, John Grant, brought us out of the field, as all the officers above him were killed, and he then took command of the regiment. His promotion to lieutenant-colonel came out from the Horse Guards about a month afterwards. That night he ordered a double allowance of grog for each man, and added that the dead men's portion might be shared among the living. So we sat round our fire, which was in the centre of a circular pit, about a foot and a half deep, and fourteen feet in diameter, and there we made as merry as circumstances would allow.

The worry of this fruitless attack added to the illness of Lord Raglan, our ommander-in-Chief, and he died ten days afterwards.

Sebastopol held out for another three months, and an attack was arranged for the 8th of September. About midday the French captured the Malakoff, but our second attack on the Redan was again unsuccessful. Our men selected for the attack were mostly recruits fresh from England, but they did their work well, even though they failed at last, for they held their ground on the loose and crumbling sides of the Russian earthworks for an hour and a half under a tremendous fire of shot, shell, and musketry.

During the ensuing night, the Russians set fire to the town, and retreated across the bay to the northern side by means of a bridge of boats. They filled many houses with gunpowder and other combustibles, and, as the fire spread, the explosions every now and then were terrific.

The siege had lasted about three hundred and forty-nine days.

I was sent into the town early the next morning with a party under one of the town-majors, or officers, appointed by our Commander-in-Chief, and I shall never forget the shocking sights we saw there. For eight months I remained in the miserable ruins of the town, upon which the Russians at first kept up a cannonade from the forts in that part of the town across the water into which they had retired.

Our release came either at the end of May or the beginning of June 1856. Seven years later, the regiment being then at Belfast, I took my discharge, having served for twenty-one years and two hundred days. My pension was eightpence a day, and would have been eightpence halfpenny if I had completed the twenty-second year. I had received the Crimean medal with three bars, the Turkish medal, and a Good Conduct medal, which last carried with it a gratuity of five pounds. For sixteen years I had been clear of a regimental entry, and this good conduct entitled me to four stripes on my right arm, and thus increased my pension fourpence a day.

Tommy Atkins' War Stories: 3

With the Guards in Egypt

By Private Macaulay

Scots Guards

Private Macaulay describes his
experiences in Egypt at the
battle of Tel-el-Kebir
and in Suakim

With the Guards
in Egypt

I joined the Scots Guards at Glasgow in 1879, and was sent to Caterham, the Recruiting Depot for the Guards, where I remained for about six months, finding the life very different from what I had expected.

When I arrived at Chelsea, I was put on the staff in the tailor's shop, where we were employed in making, repairing, and altering uniforms, for which work we received additional pay.

With the exception of my marriage, nothing eventful happened to me till about July 1882, when we were warned for active service in Egypt. The order came so suddenly that no furlough was granted to enable us to bid our friends goodbye.

In consequence of this, thousands of people assembled in front of the barracks by three o'clock in the morning of the 29th July, the day on which we were to embark. There were among them, wives, mothers, sisters, brothers, fathers, friends, children, and relations belonging to the officers and men, all anxious to see us off. Amidst the greatest excitement and enthusiasm, we were marched to Westminster Bridge Pier, where there were, I think, four steamers waiting to take us down the river. Such crowds of people I had never seen before; they lined the streets as we passed along, and increased in numbers every moment. They flocked with us to the Embankment and the Bridge, and watched our embarkation with much interest.

When at last we began to move off, the cheering was deafening, and, as we passed down the river, we noticed that the Embankment from Westminster Bridge to Blackfriars was packed with sightseers. Every bridge under which we passed was crowded to watch our progress, and when at last we had left London behind us, many people took train for Gravesend, and, by the time we came in sight of the town, they were out on the river in small boats to see the last of us.

We embarked on the Oriental Steam Navigation Company's steamer Orient, which was in the river awaiting our arrival. There were upwards of seven hundred men in our battalion, which was under the command of Colonel Knox. The Duke of Connaught also embarked at the same time, and several members of the Royal Family came on board to bid him goodbye.

We had splendid weather during the voyage. I believe I saw only a few men sea-sick, and they soon recovered. We amused ourselves with smoking, reading, and card-playing, and had a smoking-concert or two, and in twelve days arrived at Alexandria.

We did not disembark for two days, and then we marched through the streets to the station, noticing on our way that many of the houses had been demolished by the shells from our ironclads. We saw very few natives in the town, as most of them had taken flight.

We took train for Ramleh, a distance of four or five miles, but the Coldstreams and Grenadiers marched there. On arriving, we pitched our tents and stationed outposts. Near our camp were two large houses ransacked by Arabi's followers, who had been all over the ground before our arrival. On one of these houses some Engineers fixed an electric search-light, and a warship, anchored just off the shore, also threw a light across the country, right up to the enemy's earthworks at Kafr Dowar.

While we were stationed here we had an opportunity of bathing in the sea, and a pioneer of the Coldstream, in diving, struck his head upon a rock below the water and was killed. This, was our first casualty. He was buried in a box, hastily made for the purpose, but it had no lid -- I don't know why; economy perhaps: I stood by the graveside while the chaplain read the Burial Service. We had no firing party, and from the whole of the surroundings we began to realise that we were on active service.

After four or five days, the whole of the brigade of Guards was ordered to prepare to march; we were not told our destination, but afterwards found we were once more going on board the Orient. After a few hours at sea, escorted by ironclads, we found ourselves in Aboukir Bay; and, on arriving there, the war vessels formed a line between the troopships and the shore, all ready for action, but none of the enemy were seen. In the evening, as usual, at eight o'clock, we slung our hammocks and turned in; but, on turning out in the morning, we found ourselves out of sight of land, and making for Port Said.

We entered the Suez Canal towards evening, and at sunset pulled up and made fast to the bank, as no ships are allowed to travel in the canal after sundown. I was disappointed in the canal, for, after having heard so much about it, I expected to find it much wider and grander. On preparing to continue our voyage down the canal, we found that the ship in front of us was aground, and would remain immovable until part of the troops on board had disembarked.

This delayed us for about an hour, after which we steamed at half-speed to Ismailia, where we arrived in the evening of the 21st August, and spent the following day in disembarking troops, baggage, officers' horses, and munitions of war. The scene was very animated, the whole of the troops landing here, a gunboat having been previously despatched to clear the coast by shelling the enemy, who had in consequence retired inland. On the 23rd of August, the day of our departure, our men captured nineteen Greeks in the act of pillaging in the town, ten of whom were afterwards shot, I believe.

We remained at Ismailia, under the shelter of the trees growing by the side of the fresh-water canal, until the afternoon of the 23rd, when at dinner-time the Duke ordered us to get under arms at once, as the enemy had attacked our advance party at El Magfas.

We started off with all speed, and marched across a long stretch of shifting sand, on which our feet slipped backward at every step. The hot wind that was blowing made us terribly thirsty, and soon the pint and a half of water which each of our water-bottles held was exhausted. Still we pushed on, as we heard plenty of firing away in front of us. At last our thirst was almost unbearable, and just then was the only time in my life when I felt I had seen enough of this world. Fortunately, however, we came in sight of a pool, into which many of us were tumbled, so eager were the men to get a drink and push on again. On arriving at the scene of action, however, we were only in time to have a few shells over our heads, and then the enemy fled.

We passed the night lying down in skirmishing order, with here and there a sentry on the lookout. We had been hot enough during the day, but when the sun had disappeared we found ourselves terribly cold, and having no overcoats, we felt it still more. At daybreak next morning, the 24th August, we started in pursuit of the enemy, whom we found strongly intrenched at Tel-el-Mahuta, where the railway and Sweet-water Canal pass through a deep cutting. With the earth and sand from their trenches they had craftily blocked up the canal, with the idea of stopping the supply of fresh water at Ismailia; and in addition to this they had thrown into the stream a number of dead bodies, both of men and camels, and, to a certain extent, had thus poisoned the water.

About half-past six our artillery came into action, firing at the enemy on the banks of the canal, while we made for their trenches; but they fled at the sight of us. General Drury Lowe went out with some cavalry and horse artillery to try and capture some trains which were waiting on the railway, running parallel with the canal, to take Arabi's troops farther up the country. We could see them crowding in the carriages, and those who were not fortunate enough to get places in the train fled along the canal and railway banks, throwing away their arms and ammunition, while our artillery peppered them as they ran.

One of the Horse Guards, who had dismounted to take an Egyptian prisoner, was attacked by him with a dagger and wounded in the hand, but, with a single side stroke, he cut his antagonist in two, and took the dagger as a souvenir!

That night we encamped on the position held by the enemy in the morning, and we lay down to sleep just as we had marched, without a greatcoat or blanket to warm us. In the stillness of night, one of the men had the nightmare or something, and started a roar which roused every man in the camp. We made a rush for our arms, expecting by the noise and confusion that the enemy had attempted to retake their position, on which they had expended a vast amount of labour. I can't help laughing when I think of one of our men who slept near me, and had taken the precaution to get inside a biscuit-sack for warmth; he was lying on an embankment, and at the first alarm jumped up, forgetting the sack that enveloped him, and, in consequence, fell down, and rolled a considerable distance before he could stop himself. It was said that the man who caused the alarm, if found, was to be shot, but he was never discovered.

Our brigade spent about a fortnight here, cutting the dams constructed in the canal by Arabi's troops, which was no easy task, especially the work in the water.

On the morning of the 28th a party of twenty of us, with three officers, a sergeant, and two corporals, one of whom drove the regimental transport which accompanied us, set off to Kassassin to obtain some provisions from the Life Guards, who were then there. The journey of ten miles across the desert under the burning sun was very trying. If we stayed to rest, the heat of the sand was so excessive that we could not lie down upon it, unless we were lucky enough to find a little patch sheltered by a bit of rock.

The way was marked by the bones or dead bodies of the Guards' horses; we passed about thirty of them, upon which the vultures had fed, or were feeding. They are not dainty birds, and leave no crumbs. The war was a blessing to them while it lasted; I can't think where they looked for food when it was over.

On arriving at our destination, an officer came out to meet us, who was a friend of one of our officers, and he kindly took all our water-bottles and got them filled for us. They were then too heavy for him to carry, so he brought them to us on the back of a small mule. He took our officers away with him to get some refreshment, and called one of the cooks and asked him to give us something to eat. I well remember what he set before us -- it was some sort of hash, or stew, made with some stuff captured from the Egyptians. We were all very hungry, and some of us made a hearty meal, but the sergeant said, "Mack, I shouldn't go too deeply into this stuff, for I don't half like the look of it." Several of us were of his opinion, and accordingly ate very sparingly.

Having loaded up our transport, we started on our return journey about four o'clock, and we had not got a hundred yards before the Guards were mounted and starting off in the opposite direction, where we soon heard heavy firing. We pushed on as fast as the shifting sand would allow, expecting every moment to see Arabi's troops appear on our left flank.

To add to our troubles and anxiety, the meal we had eaten began to upset us, and two or three of the men had to be helped along by the others, and at last one was utterly unable to move a step farther. This set the colonel "grousing," but Sir William

Gordon Cumming got us out of our difficulty by dismounting and putting the man on his horse. We were thus enabled to struggle on to our camp, arriving in the dusk of the evening, feeling that the twenty miles we had just marched were equal to fifty in England.

Footsore and weary, we dispersed to our respective companies, and I flung myself on the ground to eat a biscuit, anticipating a good night's rest, but, to my great surprise, the order was given for all the men to get under arms, and prepare to march to Kassassin. The Colonel, who had accompanied us, called out, "Any man who thinks he is unable to do the march may go to the hospital," which was a little native church on the banks of the canal, capable of holding about twenty or thirty people, over which it was intended to place a guard of about forty men.

Thinking it safer to go with the main body than to remain behind, with the chance of an attack by the enemy, I filled my bottle at the canal, pulled myself together, put a pebble in my mouth to allay my thirst, and started off. "When we had got four or five miles on the way, we met a mounted orderly, who told us the battle was over, and our services were not required. We therefore halted for a short time, and then retraced our steps. Many of the men had emptied their water-bottles, but, thanks to my pebble, mine was not more than half empty when we reached our old camping-ground.

The next day we resumed our work at the canal, and continued till about the 8th of September, when we again marched over the trackless waste to Kassassin, where we arrived in time to hear of another battle just over. We were served out with water as though it were grog, and we had to make the most of it. The bullocks, which had been brought with us under the charge of the Commissariat Department, were killed, shared out, cooked, and eaten, and we were on the march again in five minutes less than two hours, to a place allotted to us about a mile off. We spent the night quietly enough, but before daybreak half the men of the battalion were placed on outpost duty on the scene of the previous day's fight, and I had to assist in burying the dead, which was not a very difficult matter, as we simply had to cover them with a few inches of sand.

Three days later, as a battle was expected, we were instructed to form the front fighting line. Before dusk we collected all the dried brushwood we could find, and having lighted several large fires, we started on a forced march to Tel-el-Kebir, leaving the fires burning to deceive the enemy. We were allowed to smoke on the first portion of the march, but, after the second halt, we lighted our pipes inside our helmets, so as not to be seen by the enemy.

Somehow or other, in the darkness, the Highland Brigade was marched in front of us, and we could never find out how it was managed, nor for what reason.

That forced march was something to be remembered. The darkness was intense, and we couldn't see where we were putting our feet, but marched on over the yielding sand, many of us worn out and half asleep. When the final halt was called, we lay down where we were, and myself and many others fell asleep. But we were soon awakened by a shot on the extreme right of Arabi's position, then one in the centre, followed by another on his left, and then suddenly the whole line opened fire; and there we stood in the darkness, awaiting orders, while the Highland Brigade, after firing several volleys, charged the position, and carried it at the point of the bayonet.

In the grey light of the morning, I saw what was to me the strangest sight my eyes ever rested on, for the sand in front of us looked as though a hailstorm was in progress, and the men marvelled at what appeared to be every foot of ground struck, except the spot upon which we stood. I looked round in amazement, wondering why we did not fall, but saw only two or three go down.

That is all I saw of the fight, and, when the enemy retreated, my battalion marched for their ground by the canal, accomplishing the distance of nearly six miles in a few minutes under an hour, for we were terribly thirsty. Every man carried seventy rounds of ammunition and two days' rations, while some, in addition, carried a small shovel.

The rebels that escaped with their lives got away by a bridge across the canal at this point, while some took to the water rather than await their turn, but our artillery kept up such a heavy fire upon them that I saw heaps of mangled dead lying upon the camp side of the bridge, along the banks, and in the water, which, in consequence, was so foul that, if at home, we should have scorned to put our feet in it, but now we were glad to drink our fill, and it seemed to me the most delicious water I had ever tasted.

Again refreshed, I had an opportunity to look round, and saw some amusing sights among our light-hearted men, for, there being a large number of camels straying about, many of the men laid claim to them, each man taking and marking his own camel, and the whole of those who had captured camels were soon riding about like so many boys released from school.

The motto with us was "Keep with the crowd," but I strolled about among the dead, overcome by the horrors that surrounded me. I came upon a body lying by itself, partly covered with a shawl, and though I had no arms with me I foolishly allowed my curiosity to prompt me to remove the shawl to see who the man was, for by his dress I saw he was of superior rank. I was surprised to find him a man between sixty and seventy years old, hiding from our men, and the pitiful look he gave me moved me to re-cover his face, and I left him there. Shortly afterwards I noticed another poor soul, belonging to Arabi's troops, who was being led to the doctor by some of our men. His was the worst case I ever witnessed; a piece of a shell had carried away the whole of the flesh from his face, and his head was covered by some of the horrible flies which infest the country. We had plenty of doctors, and they attended to the wounded of the enemy, but our stretcher-bearers were all clever fellows, and were able to attend to the unimportant casualties.

We spent the night and the following day at the place, during which time I entered the store of Arabi's army, and from amongst the large assortment of goods I found there, I was content to take only a towel and a clean starched, full-fronted white shirt.

About six in the evening we got into the train at the curious little station of Tel-el-Kebir, and spent the cold and cheerless night travelling in carriages which were like cattle trucks, and about ten in the morning we arrived at Cairo, marching in at the front gate of the citadel, while Arabi's troops went out at the back.

Here we stayed for a month or so, and then proceeded to Alexandria, where we embarked, and arrived at Portsmouth on November 14, 1882. We remained in London till February 1885, when we were ordered to proceed to Suakim, and accordingly embarked at Gravesend for the voyage.

We found Suakim held by a few English troops who had arrived before us, and were employed in keeping Osman Digna's troops at bay, for they made it their business to attack the camp every night. However, they let us have a quiet night to begin with, but on the second night, shortly after dark, a few shots were fired at us, and replied to by our outposts. Every succeeding night witnessed small skirmishes with the enemy, who crawled on the ground like snakes, and some often came silently near enough to stab our sentries. One managed to pass the sentry and entered the guard tent, where the men off duty were sleeping, and he slashed about him right and left with a double-edged sword, but was soon shot.

This sort of thing continued until it was decided to attack

the enemy's position in the mountains at Hasheen, previous to which the gunboat Dolphin had made it hot for them when they came to the wells for water by day, and at night she threw the search-light about the desert, and this was beyond their comprehension, for we learned from prisoners whom we afterwards captured that they could never understand it.

"When the time came to attack them in the mountains, all the troops formed up, leaving only enough men behind to guard the camp. We marched in square, with the cavalry scouting, and coming to the hills, we found their crest occupied by the enemy. Our cavalry then went forward to draw them down, while our artillery attempted to get a gun to the summit; of a small hill, from whence they could command the neighbouring heights, but, unluckily, they had not ascended more than about a dozen yards, when the gun toppled over, and some of the men and horses were thrown upon the ground. The excitement was intense, for the enemy were coming down upon our cavalry like wild dogs; and were led by two chiefs mounted on a white camel.

Seeing the accident, the cavalry did not return until they saw the gun righted and dragged within the square, when they immediately followed, and the whole face of the square fired a volley at the advancing multitude.

Among the first to fall were the two men from the camel, and there was something very laughable in the way they went over, but what was more remarkable was that the camel did not fall, but set off at full gallop along the face of our square, and although hundreds of the enemy were falling before the storm of bullets, yet that camel disappeared from view galloping as fast as he could go.

Our fire soon checked the advance of the enemy, but a number of them had taken up a position on a hill to our left, and the marines and a battalion of Sikhs were ordered to drive them

off at the point of the bayonet. This they did in gallant style, sending them flying across the desert towards Tamai, where our cavalry were waiting to charge them on the plain, and not one of them escaped.

All this time we were being peppered from the hills by their sharpshooters, and several men were killed, among them Captain Dallison of our battalion, who was shot through the heart. I believe the action lasted about four hours, but as it was useless holding the position, we withdrew for about a mile and a half, and had some sort of a dinner, leaving three guns, and, I think, the 50th Regiment to guard the wells at the foot of the hills. As the enemy again took up a position on the hills, our artillery opened fire on them and cleared them out, but the whole day's work did not accomplish much, and we returned to camp at Suakim, tired out after our exertions; and here we remained for some time.

On the 22nd of March, when I was doing outpost duty on one of the redoubts, I saw General MacNeill pass with about three battalions of troops, on their way to make a zereba on the road to Tamai. Some time during the day, while they were thus engaged, we heard rapid firing, which was at once a signal for us to get under arms, and we were formed up, and marched towards the spot from whence came the sound of firing, which seemed to indicate hot work. We were pushing on rapidly, when a heliograph message was received to the effect that the fighting was over, and we thereupon turned back.

The following few days were very trying, for we had to pass to and from the zereba every day, marching over shifting sands which scarcely covered the recently-slain enemy, whose legs and arms could be seen sticking out in all directions, with here and there a vulture tearing off the putrefying flesh.

Soon after, there was a general move made for Tamai, which we reached just about sundown. We bivouacked in a valley.

Some of us were told off to set fire to the village, and it was all ablaze in about ten minutes, but, as the enemy had placed ball cartridges in the thatch of the houses, the work was rather risky. Others had to fill up the wells, and the rest of us replied to the enemy's fire, and eventually drove them from their position; when we retired to the zereba to pass the night.

On our return to Suakim we embarked on the *Jumna* for Kamleh, where we spent a fortnight, and then re-embarked for Cyprus. We remained on the island for about six weeks, and afterwards sailed for England, arriving about the end of August; and a fortnight afterwards I was transferred to the Reserves, giving God thanks for my safe deliverance, and having seen enough of the glories and horrors of war.

Tommy Atkins' War Stories: 4

The Charge of the Six Hundred

By Joseph Grigg

4th Light Dragoons

Joseph Grigg offers a unique account of the Charge of the Light Brigade at Balaklava and relates an early incident in the career of Gordon of Khartoum.

The Charge of the Six Hundred

My father was a soldier at the time of the Battle of Waterloo, but he had at that time to do duty in Ireland.

As a boy, I always had a desire to see a battlefield, and made up my mind to enlist in a cavalry regiment. On the 21st October 1843, when at the age of eighteen, I joined the 4th Light Dragoons, now the 4th Hussars, at Exeter, where I was born, and where the regiment was then stationed. I enlisted for unlimited service.

We were moved to various places, at each of which we stayed, as was usual in those days, twelve months.

In 1851 I volunteered for service at the Cape, against the Kafirs, but was not accepted, as there were more volunteers than enough.

In 1853 we were stationed at Chobham, when we were ordered to march to Canterbury, and, early in July in the following year, we marched from thence to Plymouth, where we embarked for the Crimea, on board the steamship *Simla*, on the 17th and 18th. The strength of the regiment was then twenty officers and three hundred and nine non-commissioned officers and men, who were under the command of Lieutenant-Colonel Lord George Paget, whose father, the Marquis of Anglesey, lost a leg at Waterloo.

Lord George was a cool-headed, brave man, and was a great favourite with all under his command. He gave us good advice during our voyage out, and in many ways endeared himself to all of us.

Our ship had a fast passage, doing the voyage in about fourteen days, as far as I can remember, and we had good weather during the whole time. We landed at Varna, and after a while re-embarked and landed at Old Fort, near Eupatoria, on the 17th September. As we had to get our horses into boats, and bring them ashore, the business of disembarkation took some little time.

On the 20th, when in sight of the heights of Alma, we were placed on the extreme left of the line, to protect the artillery, who were on the left of the infantry; it was our duty to keep back the Cossacks in order to prevent them getting in rear of our column. We could watch the attack from where we were, and saw the Rifle Brigade and the Highlanders and Guards go up the hills like cats. Nothing but death or wounds stopped them.

We had but little to do, and only one or two of our men got slight flesh wounds. When our troops got to the top of the heights, we closed in towards the main body, but were not allowed to give chase, although the Russians were in full retreat. The fight, which began about noon, was over between three and four. We linked our horses together in long lines and set about getting things ship-shape, after which we had to take our horses down to the river for water. There is always plenty to do if you have a horse to look after. The men had been served out with three days' rations, and the horses carried provender to last them for the same period.

When we had time to look about us, we were horrified by the sight of the wounded, who lay scattered around in all directions, higgledy-piggledy as you may say; sometimes legs and arms were lying by themselves while the men were lying a little distance off. Some lay in heaps of mingled friends and foes; in other places I saw Russians and Englishmen who were grappling when death overtook them. Where shells had burst, the bodies lay scattered around; but where large shots had struck the men, they were terribly mutilated, while the bullets had struck them in all parts of their bodies. Somewhere on the hill we came upon the ruins of a grand stand. It was supposed that the ships' guns had demolished it, and that it had been erected for Russian spectators, who expected it would take six weeks for us to get up the hills.

Each regiment, as far as possible, picked up its own wounded and buried its own dead. During the two nights we remained on the battlefield our men were employed on vedette duty, and the moans of the wounded were terrible to listen to. Our men were out the greater part of the first night attending to them. They had strict orders not to plunder the dead, but I believe there was a little of it done, especially when the Russians wore earrings. The French were less particular about this than we were.

One day I was mounted with my troop, waiting for orders from Lord Raglan, who was on a hill behind us, from whence he could see the greater part of the battlefield, and send an aide-de-camp with an order whenever necessary.

From where we were formed up, we watched the enemy place nine field guns across the valley at about half a mile from us; and two field batteries of two guns each were put into position, one on a slope on the left of the guns, and one on the right. Two squares of infantry were also posted on the left of the guns, under cover of the guns on the hillside, while others were in possession of the redoubts which the Turks had deserted.

I saw Captain Nolan, of the 15th Hussars, come galloping down from Lord Raglan to where Lord Lucan and Lord Cardigan were, and we knew then that there was something for us to do.

Our men of the Light Brigade were the 17th Lancers (Duke of Cambridge's Own), as fine a regiment as ever carried lances; the 8th Hussars, a nice lot of fellows, always ready for anything in the fighting way; the 11th Hussars, who all did their duty well; the 13th Light Dragoons, as good as any in the fight; and our 4th Queen's Own Light Dragoons, who were as ready for it as the others.

The Earl of Cardigan shouted out, "The Brigade will advance -- March!" and Trumpet-Major Joy, who was orderly, sounded the "Trot" when we had got into walking order, and we then broke into a trot. Soon the trumpet sounded "Gallop," and afterwards "Charge," and away we went at a splendid pace. As we got nearer the guns our pace was terrific; the horses were as anxious to go as we were; mine snorted and vibrated with excitement, and I could hardly keep my seat, for we seemed to go like the wind.

We were in three lines: in the first, as nearly as I can remember, were the 13th Light Dragoons and 17th Lancers; second line, 4th Light Dragoons and 11th Hussars; third line, 8th Hussars. The lines were about a hundred yards apart, so that when a man went down with his horse, the man behind him had time to turn his horse on one side or jump him over the obstacle. Every man thus had all his work to do to look before him, and there were not many chances to watch the dreadful work of the shots, shells, and bullets, which were showered at us from all directions.

The first man to fall was Captain Nolan, who went clown directly we got within the range of their guns; but soon afterwards men and horses began to fall fast; the man on my right hand went down with a crash, and soon afterwards the man on my left went down also. I remember, as we neared the guns, Captain. Brown, who was in command of our squadron, called out to the men in the second line, who were getting too near the front, "Steady, men, steady! You shall have a go in directly."

Just before we got to the guns, we gave three loud cheers, and then, in a moment, we were among the enemy.

As I passed the wheel of the gun-carriage the gun was fired, and I suppose some of the 8th Hussars got that shot, or shell, or whatever it was. The wind was blowing from behind us, and the smoke from the guns prevented us from seeing very well what work there was for us to do.

The first man I noticed was a mounted driver. He cut me across the eyes with his whip, which almost blinded me, but as my horse flew past him, I made a cut at him and caught him in the mouth, so that his teeth all rattled together as he fell from his horse. I can fancy I hear the horrible sound now. As he fell I cut at him again; and then I made for another driver, and cut him across the back of his neck, and gave him a second cut as he fell.

A few gunners stood in a group with their rifles, and we cut at them as we went rushing by. Beyond the guns the Russian cavalry, who should have come out to prevent our getting near the gunners, were coming down upon us howling wildly, and we went at them with a rush. I selected a mounted Cossack, who was making for me with his lance pointed at my breast. I knocked it upwards with my sword, pulled up quickly, and cut him down across the face. I tried to get hold of his lance, but he dropped it.

As he was falling, I noticed that he was strapped on to the saddle, so that he did not come to the ground, and the horse rushed away with him. His lance, like all the others used by the Cossacks, had a black tuft of hair, about three inches from the blade, to hide a hook having a sharp edge, with which the reins of their enemies are cut when the lance is withdrawn after a thrust.

Some men of the 4th, and I, made for several other Cossacks who were there in a body, cutting our way through them as through a small flock of sheep; and while thus engaged, the batteries on the slopes fired upon us, and their own men also, which was strange warfare, to say the least of it!

Just then I heard Lord George Paget call out, "Rally on

me!" I turned and saw him holding up his sword, and we all turned our horses towards where he had taken up a position in front of the guns. On arriving there, we noticed a regiment of Polish Lancers, which had come out from an opening in the hills behind us and was preparing to charge our rear; we thereupon charged through the guns again, killing several Russian Hussars who were still there. It seemed to me then, in the terrible din, confusion, and excitement, that all the gunners and drivers were on the ground, either dead or wounded.

Before the Polish Lancers had time to form line and attack us, the Chasseurs d'Afrique (a French regiment), who were coming down the valley at a sweeping pace, drove them back with great loss.

After a short engagement with the Russian Hussars, we turned our horses in the direction of our starting-place and rode back the best way we could, under fire of the infantry and the batteries on the hills.

I was in company with a comrade belonging to my own troop, and all of a sudden down went his horse, and he pitched over its head and lay helpless on the ground. I immediately dismounted and picked him up, when I found his shoulder was dislocated. Regimental Sergeant-Major Johnson, of the 13th Light Dragoons, who was coming up behind us, rode towards us, calling out, "What's the matter?" and between us we got him back in safety.

Captain Portal, who did not get a wound, rode an Irish horse called "Black Paddy." A large piece of a shell struck it in the shoulder, and directly we got back the poor animal fell dead. The captain had the hoofs cut off and preserved. I saw them some time afterwards beautifully polished, shoes and all.

Captain Hutton, I believe, was wounded in several places, and so was his horse, which also fell dead directly it returned from the charge.

Private Samuel Parks, Lord Paget's orderly, who dismounted to pick up Trumpet-Major Crawford, was taken prisoner with several others. After thirteen months he was exchanged, and Lord George Paget asked him all about his doings. He told us that General Menschikoff said to him, "Did they make all your men drunk before the charge?" "No, sir," he answered, "unless a pen'orth of rum in an evening would do it, for we only pay a penny a day for our allowance." "Well," said the General, as he walked away, "I never saw a prettier charge in all my life."

Parks also told us that he and some others were taken to St. Petersburg, where they were well treated, and allowed eight-pence a day each for food, which was very cheap.

On the following day, General Cathcart wrote to our commanding officer for an orderly, to be sent to take the place of one of the five men who were chosen for this duty, who had fallen sick. The Captain sent me up with a letter, and from that time I acted as one of the General's orderlies.

On the afternoon of the 4th of November there was a meeting of all the commanding officers up at Lord Raglan's quarters. General Cathcart called me to him in the evening, and said, "Don't go away, Grigg; I may want you presently." Later on he called me, and said, "Do you know where Captain Gordon is to be found ?" I answered that I did not know, but would soon find him.

The General replied, "You know the windmill; go direct to it, turn to the left, and then inquire of the sentries."

The night was pitch dark when I got to where the sentry was posted. He challenged me with the usual "Who goes there?" I explained that I wanted Captain Gordon of the Engineers, and, after being passed from one sentry to another, I was at last conducted to a very little tent in the most advanced post in front of Sebastopol.

The captain was sitting all alone in his tent, with no light burning, for fear of making a mark for the Russian gunners. The sentry called gently, "Captain Gordon." "Yes," he answered, coming to the tent door; "what is it ?" "I have come from General Cathcart, sir," I answered. "Yes, and what have you got ?" he asked. "A little note for you, sir," I replied, handing him the letter.

He stepped into the tent again, struck a wax match, and read the note, and I heard him say as he read it, "Prepare for action in the morning." Then, coming to the tent door again, and speaking in a low voice, he said to me, "Tell the General, 'All right.' Good-night."

I bade him good-night and found my way back, wondering what the next day would bring forth.[1]

On arriving at the General's tent, I took up my position as usual behind it, waiting for orders. He always dressed himself ready for fighting before he lay down for the night. It was a miserable night, with a mist and fog that soaked into our clothes, and just before the day broke we heard firing in the direction of our outposts. The General came out from his tent and ordered the bugler, who stood beside me, to sound the "Assembly." The call was taken up all over the camp, and in a moment all the troops were on the move. The General mounted his horse, and I followed him.

It was not long before shot and shell were flying in all directions, and our men were moved out to meet the approaching Russians, who were creeping upon us through the dense fog. I was sent to various parts of the field with orders, and during my rides saw many shocking sights. My last order from the General was to go and bring up a French battery and post them at a certain spot, and when I returned to the Staff I found the General

---

1. This incident is interesting, touching as it does the life of one who in after years, as "General Gordon," was to become one of the most honoured of Britain's heroes.

had been in the thick of the fight and was missing. Later in the day, when we found him, he had a bullet wound in the head and three bayonet wounds in his body, and was quite dead.

As near as I can remember, it was somewhere about four o'clock in the afternoon when the Russians retreated, helter-skelter, back to their own ground round Sebastopol.

After the fight (since known as the Battle of Inkermann) I had to go to the commanding officers of the Fourth Division, to ascertain how many men were fit for night duty. I forget the exact numbers, but I know they were very much reduced.

The next few days were taken up in attending to the wounded, and burying the dead in large pits. The Turks had to do most of the burying, and had ropes to put round the bodies and drag them to the pits. Our men allowed them to treat the Russian dead that way, but made them carry the English.

I saw little of these sights, as I was always riding about on orderly duty, and every now and then I had to go down to Balaklava with letters, which I handed to a petty officer of the ship that was to take despatches to England.

These rides to Balaklava were sometimes most difficult, for the roads were so muddy that the horse would sink in up to his knees, and, as fodder was scarce, the horses were nearly dead from starvation. At first we had found large quantities of grapes at Balaklava, and even fed our horses with them, but at last matters got so bad that I have known the horses eat each other's manes and tails; and bite at the men's beards and clothing. At the best of times we only gave them two feeds a day, with only six pounds of barley each feed.

About the 20th December, I rejoined my troop at Balaklava, and took my turn with the others at outlying picket duty until the fall of Sebastopol. A few days afterwards our commanding officer gave some of us permission to go into the town to see the result of our siege. The first place I noticed was a church, which had a wooden porch built over the pathway, in which a large bell was hung, having a thick rope tied to the clapper so that a man in the street might ring it. The place appeared to be utterly deserted; the churches into which I looked were empty, with large holes knocked in the roofs through which our shots had crashed. Many shots and shells were lying in the roads, and many houses were in ruins, for the Russians had left convicts in the town to burn it down. I don't think I saw anything intact anywhere.

When peace was proclaimed, I left with others for Scutari, and afterwards sailed for England, reaching Portsmouth on the celebration of the Queen's birthday, when all our ships in the harbour were illuminated.

After spending some time at various places, I took my discharge in 1860, and in the following year joined the 5th Lancers and went to India; returning in 1869, and finally leaving the service on the 5th of June in that year, with rank of sergeant, having served twenty-five years and twelve days, and having received the Crimean medal with four clasps, the Turkish medal, and one Good Conduct medal.

Tommy Atkins' War Stories: 5

With Wolseley in Ashanti

By Geo. H. Gilham

2nd Battalion, Rifle Brigade

Geo. H. Gillman recollects his service
with the Rifle Brigade in the
jungles of West Africa and the
advance to Coomassie.

With Wolseley
in Ashanti

I enlisted at Canterbury, and joined the 2nd Battalion of the Rifle Brigade at Dover on the 11th of November 1870.

At the latter part of 1872 we spent thirty-one days under canvas on Salisbury Plain for the autumn manoeuvres, and soon afterwards proceeded to Portsmouth, where we embarked for Ireland, and after three days landed in Dublin and proceeded to Birr. After a time, as disturbances were brewing in Ashanti, and the regiment was expected to be sent out there, each man was granted six weeks' leave of absence. During the holiday I received notice to rejoin the regiment, which had been ordered to embark at Queenstown on the 10th December 1873.

On my return to the regiment we took train to Cork, where we went on board three barges and were towed down to Queenstown, and embarked in the *Himalaya*, which was awaiting our arrival.

Being a bad sailor, I was confined to my bunk for seven days. Several others were as bad, while a few were worse. The vessel stayed at Madeira for two or three hours, where officers and sergeants were allowed on shore, and they returned bringing with them half a dozen sacks of oranges for the men, being one sack for each company. My share brought me round a bit, and I was able to get on deck. After this we touched at St.Vincent; and soon afterwards put in at Sierra Leone, where we shipped seven or eight bullocks, which we killed on board and salted down in small tubs.

From here we proceeded to Cape Coast Castle, where we

arrived without adventure, and landed on the 1st of January 1874. Just before landing another troopship came in sight, and as she neared us we heard the pipes of the 42nd Highlanders, at which we were delighted, as we had been under the impression that only ourselves and the 23rd Welsh Fusiliers were to be engaged.

As the surf was running pretty high we had to proceed to the shore in surf boats, and. having got as near the beach as possible, a large number of natives came into the water and landed us on their backs. The Fantees were crowding the shore to watch our progress, and they bowed themselves to the ground before us, begging for "bacca," and wishing us, in their broken English, "A Happy New Year."

We found the castle, which has belonged to England for two hundred years, a good-sized building of stone, but the native huts which surrounded it were filthy. Now and then we came against a stench which nearly choked us. The climate being unhealthy added to the danger of disease, and we were all served out with pipes and tobacco, with orders to smoke for protection. I was not a smoker, but soon managed to learn the art.

Many of the Fantees had been drilled by the English at the Castle, but Sir Garnet Wolseley, suspecting treachery, disarmed them, except a few, who were employed as gunners with the six-pounders and Gatling gun.

The atmosphere was very thick, and the weather sultry, and we started at once up the country to a small Fantee village about seven miles inland, called Inquabim. Never having set foot in a tropical climate before, I was astonished at the splendid trees, and charmed by the dense vegetation through which we passed. As the natives had no vehicles, all the roads were simply beaten tracks through the forest; but a party of Engineers had preceded us and cleared a better path for us, so that we got on more comfortably than we otherwise should have done.

Next day we marched to Accroful, seven miles nearer the river Prah, which divided Ashanti from the Fantees' land; and here the officers in command had to put a price on fruit, upon which the natives wanted too much profit. On the following day we continued our march for about ten miles, and halted at a place called Yancoomassie. We carried seventy rounds of ammunition each, and the natives carried, our kits, and even then we were almost overpowered by the heat; and every time we encamped we had to take off all our clothes, which were drenched with perspiration, and put on those we wore the day before, which had been dried in the sun.

Every morning we were astir at half-past two, and paraded half an hour later ready to march. Our captain, on inspecting our rifles here, found a piece of rag stuck in the muzzle of mine to prevent rust, and which I had omitted to remove. For this neglect I was ordered to assist in fatigue work for three days as a defaulter.

On the fourth day, which was Sunday, we reached Mansu, about twelve miles from our last camp; and here our men discovered a Dutchman, who had brought up refreshments from the coast, and was selling ale at one and ninepence per bottle, and a bottle of lemonade for tenpence. I could not resist the temptation of leaving the camp to purchase some ale, and, being a defaulter at the time, I had my punishment extended for another two days.

Next day we were up at two in the morning, and continued our march for eleven miles, passing through dense jungle in which we could scarcely see the daylight. We spent the night at a village called Sutah, lighting large bonfires to keep off the wild animals, which we could hear in the depths of the forest.

On the 6th of January we pushed on to Yancoomassie Assin, where some of our allies gave us an exhibition of their "War Dance." The day following we reached the Prah, where we encamped for a fortnight, awaiting the arrival of the right wing of our battalion. While resting here, six or seven chiefs came in with proposals for peace, but Sir Garnet would not come to terms with them. He showed them one or two experiments with the Gatling gun, at which they were greatly astonished, and soon afterwards one of them shot himself. The others were escorted out of the camp, across the temporary bridge put up by the Engineers over the river, and then sent back to King Coffee.

On the 21st of January we paraded at 7p.m. to bury an officer, and shortly afterwards we crossed the river into the enemy's country. After a wearisome march of fifteen miles, over a road rendered exceedingly rough by the roots of the gigantic trees, and passing here and there dead bodies in advanced stages of decomposition, we halted for the night, and pitched our tents at Essarman.

The day following found us encamped fifteen miles nearer our destination, at Accrafoomu. Then on the following day we proceeded to Momsey, eleven miles nearer Coomassie. Here we saw two white men, a woman, and a child, whom the King had released after a long captivity. The march on the following day took us over the Adansi Hills, a height of about one thousand five hundred and sixty feet above sea-level. We were disappointed in the view, for we could see nothing but tree-tops. On descending the hills and entering the forest we found pieces of white rag fastened to several trees, which we took as signals of peace; and here we came upon some more chiefs who had an interview with Sir Garnet, after which they were marched out of the camp, the men lining the road, and the buglers sounding the "General Salute."

Soon afterwards we captured a prisoner, from whom the General gained some valuable information. After several days' advancing, our skirmishers, on the 31st, came upon a large body of the enemy, who opened fire upon them, causing them to fall back and rejoin the main body. Upon this we received the order, "Chin-straps down, open out, and push on through the jungle." I was one of the leading four of the front company, and as our skirmishers came in, I noticed one with the bones of his arm broken by slugs from the enemy's muskets,

"We cut our way right and left into the jungle with our cutlasses, lying down in the underwood, standing behind trees for cover, pegging in where we could, and forming a semi-circle to the front; but the foliage was so dense that it was like being in a net, and the farther we went the thicker it seemed to get, so that I don't believe we advanced a hundred yards during the whole of the fight.

The enemy were all armed with flintlock muskets, obtained from the old Dutch settlers, and they fired at us with rough bits of lead, old nails, pebbles, and rusty iron, which at first passed over our heads and showed us that the enemy were on a slope below us, whereupon we fired low and did terrible execution among them, although we could only catch sight of them here and there. Our men numbered about two thousand, while the Ashantis were believed to muster something like twenty thousand. They outflanked us on several occasions, but we changed front, first on one side and then on the other, so that we were always ready for them.

We had not long been in action before a slug crashed into the breast of a marine on my right hand. Poor fellow, I shall never forget how he fell back and curled himself up in his agony. Directly afterwards a man belonging to the Naval Brigade, on my left, was hit in the shoulder, and went down like a log. The doctors were continually passing up and down behind us, and two came along just afterwards and cut the slug from the chest of the marine, but they could not get at the bullet that hit the sailor. Both men were carried to the rear.

Soon afterwards my front-rank man, Richards, an old chum

of mine, was shot just by the side of his right eye, the bullet passing round the side of his head under the skin, and coming out at the back. I had to help him to the sick-tent, which the Engineers had hastily erected. I got back to my place in time to see an officer close to me shot through the arm, and several others were either killed or wounded near me; and, after about six hours' fighting, I got a shot just above my right hip, which caused a flesh wound about three or four inches long. I was attended to by a doctor, and resumed my firing.

A small field gun which was got into position did good work among the enemy, as did also the rockets which were sent among them, and no doubt astonished them. When at last they retreated, we went after them as well as we could, and we found that they had dragged their dead into heaps. Pressing on beyond their dead, and driving the fugitives before us, we captured their village, Amoaful. We rested here that night, but were alarmed once by the enemy making an attack upon our sick and baggage. However, we drove them off, and heard no more of them. Our losses in the fight, in killed and wounded, were -- Naval Brigade, 29; 42nd Highlanders, 114; Rifle Brigade, 23; Welsh Fusiliers, 53.

On the following day we continued our march towards Coomassie, and drove the natives from several villages through which we passed. Before we started the next morning our scouts brought in five or six chiefs who had been sent by the King with a flag of truce to ask for four days' grace, but as Sir Garnet Wolseley wanted to get us all out of the country before the commencement of the rainy season, he would not agree to their proposal, and the troops were formed up in line to see them safely out of the camp.

We rested that night on the south side of the river Dah, and spent one of the most miserable nights we had during the campaign. The thunder, lightning, and rain were incessant, and the darkness was so intense that the sentries could only be posted by the aid of a compass, a candle, and a box of matches. The heavy rain, no doubt, prevented the enemy from attacking us by damping the priming of their old muskets.

Crossing the river early the following day we encountered a large body of Ashantis drawn up to oppose us for the last time, for we were then very near the capital, and intended making short work of it. They made a good stand for a few hours, and while the fight lasted it was hot work, for the firing on both sides was terrible, but they had to give in at last and make for the bush behind the town, King Coffee going away with the first of them.

To get to the town we had to pass through a shallow river about three hundred yards wide, the water reaching a little above our knees. The General, who was going through at the same time, on a mule I think it was, said, "Come on, my lads, you will have a house to sleep in to-night, perhaps a palace." We pushed on with a cheer, and soon the British flag was flying over the miserable old town. We drove out all the natives, taking away all the arms we could find, and breaking them up. We found a good many wounded natives, whom our doctors looked after.

Our Fantee bearers, who had all along been afraid to advance into the enemy's country, were now particularly bold, and we had to keep a sharp lookout to prevent them looting, -- and on this point English discipline is always severe. The first man caught offending, after having been previously cautioned, was hung on a tree, by the General's orders. I shall never forget the poor wretch's struggles. He was soon overpowered, bound hands and feet, a rope with a slip-knot was put round his neck, and he was hoisted well off the ground. The more he struggled the worse it was for him, and there we left him as an example to the others.

Having a little time to look about the place, I went into what we called the "Skull Gallery," a mud hut, about thirty feet long and twelve feet wide. The walls were thicker at the bottoms, and cut away towards the top to form about half a dozen steps or shelves, along which were rows of skulls, placed side by side, and forming a dismal exhibition.

We found some Fantee prisoners who had been in irons for several years by order of the King, and we saw many instances of his barbarity. Skulls and bones were used as ornaments for the huts. Some were stuck on poles at various parts of the town. The war drums left behind by the native warriors were all decorated with skulls. The place of execution near the market square presented a frightful scene; it was about forty yards square, and was covered with dead bodies left to be eaten by the wild animals and vultures. There were heaps of bones, and skulls without number, and the stench arising from the decaying bodies was unendurable.

There was not much time to waste in looking about, as we were anxious to leave the country, so some of our men were told off to collect trophies, while others were set to work to undermine the King's palace, which, on the 6th of February, we blew up; and having set fire to the town, started on our journey to the coast. Although we had a large number of wounded to bring back, we managed to get over the ground much quicker than before, so that we generally accomplished two days' journey in one.

We had left parties of the two West India Regiments at each stopping-place on our way up, so that the road was open to us all the way back, and we burnt each village as we came to it, and so left nothing behind us but smouldering ruins.

At last we arrived at Cape Coast Castle, and re-embarked on the *Himalaya* on the 21st of February, arriving at Portsmouth on the 26th of March. Four days later we were reviewed by the Queen at Windsor.

Tommy Atkins' War Stories: 6

Alma, Inkermann and Magdala
By Sergeant Taffs

4th Regiment

Sergeant Taffs relates his experiences fighting in the Crimea and hospitilisation
under Florence Nightingale, followed by
the storming of King Theodore's Magdala.

Alma, Inkermann,
and Magdala

At the age of eighteen I found myself, by force of circumstances, starving in the streets of London, and determined to
tramp to Chatham and enlist as a soldier. On the 3rd of June
1853 I put on my uniform as a recruit in the 99th Regiment,
and was I very soon tired of the monotony of the life I led in
barracks.

In the following year an official communication was received,
asking for volunteers to make up the strength of the various
regiments ordered for service in the Russian War.

I jumped at the opportunity of seeing a change of life, and in
a few days those who had volunteered received orders to join
their respective regiments; and as I had chosen the 4th King's
Own, known as the "Lions of England," then stationed at Edinburgh, I started for that city, and was soon afterwards entered
on their muster-roll, with just a faint idea of being known to
posterity as a second "Coeur de Lion."

I think it was in February 1854 that our regiment embarked
on the *Golden Fleece*, then lying in Leith docks, and we sailed for
Malta, where we disembarked and encamped for a short time,
afterwards re-embarking and proceeding to Gallipoli.

We spent some time at various places in Turkey, where we
went through a course of practical trenching, under the superintendence of sappers and miners, now known as the Royal
Engineers. I remember we completed a splendid entrenched
fortification, and the knowledge we thus gained was of much
service to us when before Sebastopol.

After a while we embarked at Gallipoli, on a hired transport, for Varna; from whence we sailed to Eupatoria, a miserable and insignificant town on the coast of the Crimea, and here our miseries commenced, for we immediately experienced the inconvenience of a scarcity of water. We were glad to drink from the muddy puddles in the road along which we marched.

Before disembarking, each man was served with three clays' rations of salt pork or beef, biscuits, and raw coffee beans; and each man carried a blanket and greatcoat, and these, with a knapsack for a pillow, formed his luxuriant couch. The tot of rum at the end of each day's march seemed the only means of keeping life in us, for we were drenched by a heavy downpour the first night on shore, and had to let our clothes get dry the best way we could.

After a dreary march towards Alma, we came, on the morning of the 20th September, in sight of the heights, on which we could plainly see the Russian forces massed for action.

My regiment was placed in the reserve division, to support the others, and about noon the action commenced, and we were under fire at once. To get to the heights we had to ford the little river from which the battle took its name. We found a wooden bridge, but the Russians had carefully removed the planks from it, so that only a few of our men managed to get over dry-shod; the others waded through the water, which was not much higher than their knees.

My regiment had to follow up behind the troops who led the attack. This was a precaution against the enemy wheeling round and taking our men in the rear. However, they did not attempt this movement, and we pushed on up the hills like flies.

Many of the wounded Russians, as they lay on the ground, fired at us after we had passed them; and I heard of a sergeant who was shot by a wounded man to whom he had given some water. These cowardly and treacherous acts aroused the indignation of our men, and in consequence many wounded Russians were bayoneted who would otherwise have been left with a chance of escape; but this chance was very remote, for those who were left suffering and helpless after the fight had no comrades to take them to a place of safety, and no doctors to attend to their injuries, and it must have added to their misery to see our men cared for and attended while they themselves were neglected, and left to die where they fell.

Including officers and men, we had one thousand six hundred and thirty wounded, while the French had one thousand and eighty-seven, so that it was impossible for our men to attend to any but our own sufferers.

The scenes we witnessed on the battlefield were indeed terrible. I saw men who had died with their hands grasping the throat of an enemy, many who were torn to pieces by bursting shells; numbers lay dead without a sign of a wound, while the faces of others were distorted as though they had died in the greatest torment. They lay in all directions upon the hillside, friends and foes alike, and some of the wounded whom we moved desired to be allowed to die in peace.

I noticed that each of the Russian infantry carried a long coarse linen bag, containing a mixture of meal and brown-bread crumbs. If that was all they had to eat, poor fellows, they were considerably worse off than we were.

On arriving at the heights overlooking Sebastopol, we were set to work upon the trenches, which were intended to enable us to approach nearer the town under cover.

We had been engaged at this work about a month when the Russians attempted to seize Balaklava, which we had captured, and in the harbour of which town our vessels were anchored. The brave charge of the noble Six Hundred will never be forgotten. I saw it from a distance, but the fight was over before my regiment could arrive on the field.

After the fight we returned to our camp, and resumed our work in the trenches with a determination to bring the Russians to surrender; but they were made of tough material, and held out well, firing at us day and night, shelling our batteries, and charging down upon us time after time.

Lots of men enlisted in England to fill up the gaps in our regiments. I believe they were offered six pounds and a free kit to induce them to join. Young recruits also came out, and were put to work in the trenches, where many lost their lives before they had been away from home a month.

Fatigue parties were continually passing to and from Balaklava, bringing up wood for huts, provisions for the men, and fodder for the horses; but the roads in many places were impassable, the horses which had the duty of bringing up stores sank knee deep in the mud, many of the wretched animals were half starved, and numbers of them fell and were left to die upon the roadside.

We saw but little that happened beyond where we were stationed, as we were seldom allowed to visit other parts of the camp. Indeed, we principally learned the position of affairs from the newspapers we received from home, and in the letters from our friends in England they expressed their surprise at our ignorance of what was going on around us.

We were always in a miserable state of suspense, daily expecting to be attacked, and continually hoping that our General would order us to storm the town, and so end the struggle. There seemed very little method adopted, and no complete organisation. The Commissariat Department was a failure, and the headquarters of confusion was at Balaklava, where provisions and medical comforts were landed in large quantities, and where they remained until the war was over.

On the 5th of November, in the early hours of the morning, the Russians poured out of the town, and boldly attacked us under cover of a dense fog which enveloped our camp. This was the commencement of the memorable Battle of Inkermann, which has been called the Soldiers' Battle; for we had suddenly to take up position and defend ourselves as best we could, and our officers had to fight among the rank and file, rather than take command, for it was impossible for them to see how matters stood, except in their immediate neighbourhood. It was a terrible time; we fought behind bushes and rocks, and charged in small parties here and there, fighting all the while like fiends.

I found myself, with about a dozen comrades, surrounded by an overwhelming number of Russians. They fired at us and then rushed upon us with fixed bayonets. I was shot in the thigh, and felled to the ground with a blow from the butt end of a musket. With a yell, a company of French came to our assistance, and drove off our assailants, and I lost consciousness. When I came to my senses the stars were shining brightly, and a dead Frenchman was lying across my breast.

I managed to extricate myself, and crawl to the top of the bank and look towards the camp. Parties of men were moving about among the dead and dying, and at last I was picked up and carried to the hospital tent, where hundreds of men were awaiting the attention of the doctors.

The next day I was taken down to Balaklava, put on board ship, and taken to Scutari Hospital, one of the most abominable hospitals on the face of the earth. Miss Florence Nightingale, and a lot of English nurses, arrived about the same time, and she had plenty of patients, for all the wards were full, and the men in attendance had to come without ceremony and carry out the dead and bury them at the rate of fifty or sixty a day.

So heavy was the death-rate, and so inadequate the accommodation and ventilation of the hospital, that a sanitary commission came out from England, and matters began at once to improve. To give an idea of the discomforts of the place, I may mention that the floor boards in the upper rooms formed the ceilings for the lower ones, and when they were scrubbed the water came down upon us as we lay in our beds below. Some of the men's wounds were left so long unattended to, that those men who were able would do a good turn by picking the maggots from them. This fact is almost too bad to print, but I mention it as one of the horrors of war.

When I was sufficiently recovered I was sent home to England to regain my health; and, on the conclusion of the war, I rejoined my regiment at Aldershot, and after spending some time in Ireland we were ordered to the Mauritius. On arriving at the Cape we heard of the outbreak of the Mutiny, and one wing of the regiment proceeded to India, while I and some others had to remain with the headquarters of the regiment at Mauritius.

We afterwards proceeded to Bombay, and remained at various stations in the Presidency until we were ordered for service in Abyssinia. Three thousand five hundred of us sailed from Bombay on the 7th of October 1867, landed at Zulla on the 21st, and Sir Robert Napier, who was in command of the expedition, landed on the 4th of January 1868.

It is not often a soldier knows much about the cause of the war in which he is engaged, but I managed to learn a few facts which caused me to take additional interest in the expedition. A missionary named Stern had been beaten and imprisoned in 1863 by order of King Theodore, and on the 3rd of January 1864, Captain C. D. Cameron, the British Consul, and all the British subjects and missionaries were imprisoned and kept in chains, like criminals, for alleged insults to the King, who called himself the King of Kings. The British Government sent a Chaldee Christian named Rassam, with Lieutenants Prideaux and D. Blanc, and after considerable negotiations the prisoners were released on the 25th of February 1866, but were subsequently seized and reimprisoned.

Our work, therefore, was to release these prisoners, and teach Theodore a lesson in humanity, and we pushed forward through the country with a strong determination to do so.

We made a grand show on the march, for we employed over 14,000 camels and bullocks, 13,000 mules and ponies, about 50 elephants, and over 800 donkeys, besides the large number of natives engaged in transport work.

We arrived below Magdala on the 2nd of April 1867, and learned that the captives had been relieved of their chains three or four days previously.

A week after our arrival below Magdala, Theodore massacred about three hundred native prisoners; and the following day, which was Good Friday, his troops attacked our First Brigade, but were defeated with much slaughter at a place called Arogee. I saw very little of the fighting, as I was behind with the Medical Staff attending to the sick and wounded; but the next day I saw Lieutenant Prideaux come with a message from the King to Sir Robert Napier, who sent him back with a letter, to which the King sent an insulting reply.

On the 13th of April we bombarded and stormed Magdala, which was built on a high tableland, access to which was only possible on one side by what was called the King's Road. Theodore's troops made a pretty good stand; but when he found we were gaining the day, he shot himself with a pistol, which some years before had been sent him as a present from Queen Victoria, I saw him lying dead with the pistol beside him, and I read the inscription engraved upon it, but I forget exactly what it was.

We took possession of the town, and collected a large number of curiosities. I brought away one or two vases from the palace, and a drinking-horn which would hold about a quart.

We set fire to the place, and burnt it to the ground, on the 17th of April, and set off at once for the coast, taking the Queen and her son with us. She died on the march back, but the boy was brought to England, where we arrived about the 21st or 22nd of June.

The expenses of the war were over eight millions sterling, and having assisted the country in this pleasant little extravagance, I took my discharge.

Tommy Atkins' War Stories: 7

With the Gunners at Tel-el-Kebir

By James Wickenden

Driver, Royal Horse Artillery

James Wickenden describes the privations
of serving with the Royal HorseArtillery
in the days leading up to and
during the battle of Tel-el-Kebir.

With the Gunners at
Tel-el-Kebir

Enlisting at Canterbury in the K Battery of the B Brigade of the Royal Horse Artillery, in the latter part of 1872, I was sent to Woolwich, where the battery was then stationed. We were afterwards removed to Aldershot, and from thence to Portobello Barracks, where the battery was broken up and the men distributed, some into other batteries of the R .H. A., and others into various field batteries.

When the Egyptian War broke out, I was in the G-Battery of the B Brigade, R. H. A., which embarked at Woolwich in the hired transport *Ludgate Hill*.

On the voyage out we stopped at Malta to take in coal, and then proceeded to Alexandria, where we landed three guns under the command of Major Borrowdale; but the same day we were ordered to re-embark, and, having slung our horses aboard again, we started for Port Said, where we entered the Suez Canal and proceeded to Ismailia.

We found the place extremely lively, as all the troops were disembarking at once, and we had all our work to do to get our horses and guns ashore and prepare for marching.

The journey through the desert was terrible, our horses sinking into the loose sand at every step. The guns, too, were almost immovable in some places, and we had to literally put our shoulders to the wheel to help them forward, working like slaves in doing so.

We were only allowed a pint and a half of water each day, and that seemed to disappear by magic. Now and then we had some tinned meat and a few potatoes, but I don't believe I had a hatful of these delicacies all the time. It seemed to me that the Commissariat Department was always behind, for whenever we halted, the provisions were miles away, and had to be waited for.

The wretched horses, too, had not got over their sea voyage before they were put to hard work and short rations. We were served out with compressed corn, which was not sufficient for the poor creatures, and we had to make up the deficiency with rushes which we cut from the Fresh-water Canal.

Before we landed every man's hair was cut as short as possible, and we were each served out with a green veil and a pair of dark spectacles. Our swords were also ground on board, and then browned by burning, blade, hilt, and scabbard; and our white helmets and pugarees were stained brown, to prevent them being conspicuous in the glaring sunlight.

We marched in the cool of the evening, and during the heat of the day we lay down under gun carriages or ammunition waggons, or anywhere, for shelter from the terrible sun. A good many of the infantry fell out of the ranks, and had to be helped along by the Indian contingent, which brought up the rear, and was told off to assist the Army Hospital Corps.

We had no overcoats, and at night the cold was intense, and we felt it terribly. I shall not forget my first night ashore, for we had to get into the water to land our horses, and had to wear our clothes till they dried, and they were still wet when the cold night air came on us. We made capital beds by scraping holes in the sand, rolling ourselves in our blankets, with our helmets for pillows, and then raking the sand over us, so that we were almost buried.

The harness was never taken from the horses, so that they were always in readiness for a night attack; they were simply shackled at night to prevent them from straying; and during the day many of them were sun-struck, and had to be shot.

On the 21st of August we came upon Arabi's troops in their advanced intrenchments at Mahuta, where they had blocked up the Fresh-water Canal; but they did not make much of a stand against us, and retreated in disorder, many of them throwing away their arms and anything else that impeded their flight. They were a disorganised lot, for we found boxes of guns that hadn't been unpacked. Perhaps this was because some preferred to fight with swords or spears, but I am certain many of them didn't want to fight at all.

During the short time that they made a stand, they fired several shells, which came pretty close to us. I remember saying, "Dear, dear, that's near enough," for I thought of my wife and four children at home, the youngest only thirteen days old when I embarked at Woolwich.

After the fight at Mahuta, in which we lost about five killed and twenty-five wounded, we pushed on to Kassassin Lock, on the Fresh-water Canal, and here we rested some days, being always on the lookout for an attack.

I was groom to Lieutenant Sir Godfrey Thomas, and, in addition to my own work, had to do little jobs for him; but I was not overworked, for the officers had to rough it quite as much as the men, with the exception of a few more luxuries to eat and drink.

One evening he said to me, "I think I'll sleep here tonight, Wickenden; down by this gun." I answered, "Very good, sir"; and scraped a hole in the sand and laid his blanket in it. As a rule we could always sleep directly we lay down, but in a few moments he said, "I can't sleep here, Wickenden." "Can't you, sir?" I asked; "what's wrong, sir?" " Why there's such an abominable smell just here." "Oh, that comes from over the hill yonder, sir, where there are a few dead horses," I replied. However, I scraped a hole for him somewhere else, and while I was moving the blanket I discovered the body of a black, buried just below the

surface, which my master had exposed by twisting and turning about in his restlessness. It gave me a bit of a shock, but I called out to one of my comrades to come and look, and we had a good laugh about it.

Early one morning our outposts came galloping in, raising the alarm, and although we were in the midst of preparing breakfast, we hooked our horses to the guns, and hurried out some little distance from the camp to meet the enemy, who were about thirteen thousand strong. This was on August 24.

Their shells were falling pretty thickly, but they buried themselves in the sand without bursting, or we should have lost a great number of our men. One shell burst near me, which took off a sergeant's left leg, and another killed a driver and wounded a trumpeter; but altogether we were very fortunate, and when we got our range we saw the enemy fall before our shells like the cutting down of rushes, for they seemed to be ten to one against us, and stood in vast crowds like sheep.

The fight lasted, off and on, all day, up to about eight or nine, as far as I can remember; but the whole fight was so exciting that we took no heed of time or hunger.

When at last we returned to camp, and were preparing tea, -- for Sir Garnet had stopped our allowance of rum, -- I was busy near some of the Indian troops, who were seated round a fire preparing a sort of pancake, when all of a sudden, bang! went a shell that had buried itself in the sand just under where they had lighted their fire. One poor fellow was immediately killed, but the others ran away howling like dogs.

We advanced towards Tel-el-Kebir, over the desert, in line, with cavalry and infantry on either side of us, and saw many of the enemy's wounded whom it was impossible to assist. They were a most treacherous lot, and hamstrung some of our horses with knives like pruning hooks. One of the horses belonging to my gun was so treated, and had to be shot by our Farrier-Major.

It was about half-past one in the morning of the 13th of September that we started to attack Tel-el-Kebir, six miles distant from Kassassin, and we proceeded as silently as possible. No smoking was allowed as we neared their position. It was still dusk when they discovered us, about a mile from them, and opened fire on us. The work of driving them from their intrenchments was left to the infantry, who advanced most gallantly in the face of a heavy but reckless fire. With a rush and a howl of defiance they charged over the earthworks with fixed bayonets, and we could hear the din of battle as we dragged our guns round the intrenchments, to harass the rebels in their retreat and add to their confusion.

The fight did not last more than half an hour, but in that time we killed or wounded two thousand of the enemy, and took somewhere about three thousand prisoners, with sixty guns and a lot of ammunition and stores.

We lost nine officers and forty-five men killed, and twenty-two officers and three hundred and twenty men wounded. This fight brought the Egyptian campaign to an end, as Arabi's troops soon afterwards laid down their arms, and Arabi, with many of his officers, was taken prisoner.

We were marched to Cairo, and some of us were stationed at Abbasieh Barracks, where I saw Arabi a prisoner. I think these barracks were the dirtiest places I was ever in. Although we had captured plenty of soap, we had very little served out to us; and what with heat and dust and filthy flies, we had about one hundred and fifty men suffering from ophthalmia. I never saw so many flies in all my life; they would settle on our eyes and lips, as it was too hot to wear our veils, and while standing talking to a comrade we had to keep our hands moving before our faces to drive them off. I used to wonder what the place could have been like when the plague was on.

We could get no straw for our horses to lie on in the stables, and they had to stand on flagstones day and night. We used to lose about fifteen or sixteen a day, and had to drag them out some distance from the barracks, where the vultures would pick their bones clean by the next morning.

The Egyptian troops, as far as I saw, were a dirty and disreputable lot. They lived like chickens, picking their food out of a large bowl, round which they sat and ate. They each received twopence-halfpenny a day, with which they had to keep themselves; and they only had meat on Fridays.

We had to go out under canvas for some time, and shift our position every now and then, which is called cholera dodging; and I would rather be in action than at that game. We lost a good many men. In my tent there were nine of us, and in one night we lost five of them. It's a dreadful experience to be talking with a chum, when he is suddenly seized with pains, and you help to get him to the hospital tent, and see no more of him until you have to assist in burying him, while an officer reads the Burial Service.

I was truly thankful to leave Egypt, and more so to land at Portsmouth on the 3rd of June 1884. We proceeded to Woolwich, where I took my discharge, after twelve years' service, for which, unfortunately, I received no pension.

Tommy Atkins' War Stories: 8

Russian Guns and Indian Rebels

By Gunner and Driver Cox

Royal Artillery

Cox saw action in the Crimea and then
in India, both at Cawnpore after the
massacre and in Lucknow during the
Indian Mutiny.

Russian Guns and
Indian Rebels

I enlisted, as a gunner and driver, in the Royal Artillery, at Canterbury, on the 20th of September 1853; and at the time of the declaration of war with Russia my battery was stationed at Woolwich.

We embarked on board the steamship *Commandant* at the Dockyard, on the 10th of June 1854, and after an uneventful voyage, except running aground at Constantinople and getting afloat again at the full tide, we reached Varna, and spent some little time in practising embarking and disembarking guns and horses.

While stationed here I had witnessed for the first time the flogging of a comrade, which had such an effect upon me that I fainted. However, I became accustomed to this brutality long before I left the service.

We afterwards proceeded to Eupatoria, where the vessels anchored in three long lines. I shan't forget noticing several bodies of persons who had died, and had been sewn up in blankets and launched overboard, floating about round the sides of the vessels, as the shots put in to sink them were not sufficient for the purpose; and this was the beginning of the shocking scenes with which we were soon to become acquainted. I remember a poor chap dying on our ship, and I had to go with others in a boat and drop him overboard beyond the outer row of ships. There was no sort of funeral service about that time, and we soon got used to the terrors of death, and were as experienced in funerals as the oldest sexton that ever lived.

The night we landed in the Crimea was a boisterous one, and we had no shelter but our greatcoats all the time. The second night was much better, but we had a false alarm, which caused a great deal of confusion throughout the whole of the force, -- Turks, French, and English.

The Russians expected the first battle would be all in their favour, and that it would probably decide the war. They had a splendid position on some hills overlooking a large plain, with a shallow river winding at the foot of them. We could see them in the distance, and went forward all excitement and determination, with the thought of having them out of it uppermost in all our minds. As we got nearer, the order was, "Cavalry in rear, and Rifles to advance in skirmishing order"; and when we were within range, the first gun was fired at us about twelve o'clock.

The artillery had all their work to do to get the guns across the river, for they sank deeply in the mud, and we had to work like horses to get them out and into position on the other side. Mine was a twenty-four pound howitzer, and, just after we commenced firing, No. 6 man, who was coming up in rear of the gun, with a shell under one arm and a cartridge under the other, was picked off with a musket ball. I took up what he had dropped, and we did as well as we could without him. It was a case of every man for himself, and we could have rendered him no assistance even if he had been alive.

General Strangeways, who was near us at the time, said to our officer, "We seldom saw a gunner fall in the Peninsula, but there are plenty falling here."

We limbered up, and advanced again into the din and confusion of the fight; and when the order was again "Action front," we found one of our gunners seated on the trail plate without his head, and holding on to the guard-iron with a death grip. A shell had taken his head off without our noticing it, and we had to loosen his hands, and lift his body down, before we could unlimber the gun.

Then came the uphill work, which was very trying, and one of our lieutenants was killed as we were struggling up, but when we reached the top the Russians were in full retreat, leaving knapsacks and other things piled up in heaps. One of their general's carriages was left just where we were, and Bombardier Graham, who was a very jolly fellow, got inside it for a joke.

We should have liked to have followed the retreating army, but it was impossible to leave all our wounded on the field, and our cavalry, who had been kept out of range, were too late to be of any service. The battle was over in three hours and twenty minutes.

The fighting, and the sights I saw around me, so overcame my appetite that it was some days before I could eat anything.

A day or two afterwards, when we marched to attack Balaklava, we found only a few soldiers and a Russian general in the castle there, who soon hoisted a flag of truce, and we took them all prisoners and put them on board one of our ships to be taken to England. After this we marched towards Sebastopol; and my battery took up a position on the right attack, close to the windmill, which we converted into a magazine.

When the Engineers had got the first trenches dug, by working for several nights at them, they continued to work like moles, cutting the trenches zigzag, and so getting gradually nearer the town. It was only necessary to put a hat on a stick and elevate it just above the top of the trench to get half a dozen bullets at it, for the enemy watched us like cats. But it was cats against bulldogs, for we went at the work with a will, although the hardships, both for men and officers, were very great.

Our battery had a furnace which we brought from Woolwich for the purpose of making our shots red-hot, and the way the chimney of that furnace got knocked about by the enemy's musket shots was wonderful. We also had thirteen-inch shells filled with a composition like Greek fire, but neither the red-hot shots nor the shells were much use against the Russians' stone batteries and earthworks.

On one occasion a shot from the enemy fell upon a heap of these shells, and set fire to the lot, making a grand blaze which it was impossible to quench, so we had to let it burn out.

The attacks on the trenches were pretty frequent, and so sudden, that I remember on one occasion five of our men were bayoneted while they lay asleep. The fire of the Russian batteries often dismounted our guns, and we had to mount them in the night following so as to be ready for action in the morning. Sometimes their fire was so well directed that their shots lodged in the muzzles of our guns.

The embrasures of our battery were often knocked about, and one day I heard a corporal order two sappers to repair them. General Gordon, who was then a lieutenant, overheard the command, and said, "Don't tell a man to do what you wouldn't venture to do yourself," and then he set to work with a shovel. I fancy I can see him now covered with dust and dirt.

One night the Russians stripped one of our dead, and next morning we saw the clothes they had taken stuck on a pole on the Redan. I suppose it was done to annoy us.

All one Saturday night, I remember, some of us had to assist the French in mounting their guns. When we looked over the parapet, the Russians, who were always on the lookout, let fly at us, and as some of us were rather venturesome, the Frenchmen called to their captain to prevent us from doing so, as some of the shots might have hit them. They seemed rather a nervous lot, and as we left them about two or three o'clock on Sunday morning, we had to have a Frenchman to guide us and prevent their sentries firing at us.

I liked their Zouaves very much; they were fine men for

fighting. Some of their sergeants spoke English well. Once a young trumpeter belonging to our battery had been down to Balaklava, but, having had too much to drink, lay helplessly at the side of the road. I happened to be coming by and heard one of them tell some of his men to carry him inside the lines for safety. He said to me in capital English, "Though he is not a countryman of mine he is a comrade of mine."

Once, in digging the trenches, it was necessary to cut through a part of the ground where a lot of men had been previously buried. The Engineers, on whom this duty fell, had a horrible job, and were under the command of Lieutenant Gordon.

During the siege a good many of the Russians deserted to our lines. Once five Poles came in together; they made us understand that many others would come but were afraid we should shoot them. We took them all prisoners, and I don't suppose they were treated worse then than when they were free.

But what was strangest to me was that some of our own men went over to the enemy. I remember a bugler of the 7th Fusiliers deserting, and the men firing at him as he ran away. Whether he was knocked over or not I don't know. One of our gunners also deserted, and the following day our mortar bed was dismounted twice. Captain Peel, one of our naval officers, said, "You've only that man to thank for it; he knows the position of your guns." Well, we were on the watch for the man who fired, and presently we saw him get up on their ramparts, to see what execution had been done, and one of our sharpshooters, who had been waiting his opportunity, picked him off nicely.

We witnessed many terrible scenes of suffering among our men. I remember, in particular, a chum of mine who was stooping down to pick up something, when a shell burst close to him and blew off both his legs and arms. I was just going to fire when they told me I was wanted, and I found the poor fellow had just been put on a stretcher. He could not speak, but I shall never

forget the expression of his eyes when I put my flask to his lips.
I covered him over with a bit of old blanket, and returned to my
duty; and when I was relieved, about two hours afterwards, the
poor fellow was still alive. The doctors could do nothing for him
but tie his veins up. On another occasion, two men were burying a comrade, when a shot from the enemy killed one of them,
and the man who was left laid the two bodies in the grave, and
completed the funeral alone.

The Russians had possession of some quarries, from which
they procured stone to build their forts, but we dug a trench
into it and had a tremendous fight for the place. At the conclusion of it, a flag of truce was hoisted by the English, and we went
out to collect our dead and wounded.

I was pretty well forward, with some sailors, and we were
looking about us to learn the position of their guns, when one
of their officers came up and kicked up such a row that we had
to clear off; but one of the sailors called out to him, "We'll give
you one presently, master."

In many places, and particularly round the Redan, the Russians had dug mines, and had set trap-fires, so arranged that if
one of us had kicked against a wire we should have exploded
the mine. We used to dig these traps up when we charged down
upon them, but it was risky work.

Most of our wounded were taken to a large hospital at Scutari, opposite Constantinople, and here, at last, they became so
numerous that the doctors were unable to attend to them properly, and the nursing staff was totally inadequate. It was at this
time that Miss Florence Nightingale, who had acquired experience in nursing at various Continental hospitals, volunteered
to come out to render assistance; and this she did, at the head
of thirty-seven ladies, who had also volunteered. They reached
Scutari on the 5th of November, the day on which the Battle
of Inkermann was fought. Their valuable aid was most welcome,

and they worked splendidly. Another hospital was established at Kululee, and the patients in the two numbered four thousand. Fifty other ladies came out from England, and, by their assistance, the whole of the wounded were carefully and tenderly nursed.

When fighting in the trenches we lost a great many men, and, having no stretchers, we dug shallow graves within the trenches and took the dead by their legs and arms and laid them in them. I remember, on one occasion, a comrade was killed, and after digging his grave I endeavoured to get possession of a splendid pair of boots he had on, but as I could only succeed in getting one off, I helped to put him in his grave, and laying the boot beside him, I buried it with him.

On the morning of 5th November we were turned out about five, and in the darkness and fog we put our horses in and marched our guns into position on the right of a ravine, to oppose the advance of the main body of the Russians, who were approaching in that direction. We were under the command of Colonel Fitz Mayor, and P Battery was on our left.

Some of the Russian artillery had taken up a position opposite us, on the other side of the ravine. We kept up a continual fire on them, and on the advancing thousands of grey-coated Russian infantry. The loss of life was fearful on both sides, our only consolation being that we suffered less than they did. The din of the battle was beyond description. We shifted our position now and then, when ordered; and later in the day some artillerymen harnessed themselves to two eighteen-pounders, drew them into position near us, and these, being heavier than ours, did good execution, and I have always believed that they checked the fight to a very great extent.

About ten o'clock I got an awful crack on the head from a splinter of a Russian shell, causing a long flesh wound; but being attended by a doctor of the 19th Regiment, who bandaged my head with lint, I was soon sufficiently recovered to continue my work at the guns. Many of our fellows were cut to pieces, others had marvellous escapes. I saw a driver belonging to my battery who had his horse shot under him, and, while he was cutting the traces, another shot killed the off horse, yet the man did not get a scratch.

General Strangeways, who had his leg shot off, was lifted from his horse and carried to the camp by four infantry men. I was told that he ordered each of them to be paid ten shillings, but when we got back to camp he was dead, and I don't suppose the men sent in a claim for the money.

After the fall of Sebastopol, or perhaps it was before it, General Dakers, I believe it was, served out the Crimean medals, and others for distinguished conduct. I remember a man who had worked at the guns at Inkermann was entitled to one, and at the time of the distribution he was a prisoner awaiting sentence for drunkenness. He was brought up to receive the medals, and marched back to the guard tent, where he pinned them on his breast. He was again marched out to receive his sentence, which was fifty lashes. This was the second time he had been flogged, and to show his bravery he took off his clothes unaided. His coat was laid over the wheel of a gun carriage, and he was lashed to the wheel, with his chin resting upon his coat. The man who was to give him the first twenty-five lashes was, at the tenth stroke, sent to the guard tent by the commanding officer, for not doing his duty properly, but was let off further punishment.

Our doctor, whose name was Barker, gave B Battery a lamb as a pet; he had purchased it at Balaklava, or had had it given him I suppose. It grew to a great size, and we made it a pewter medal, and taught it lots of tricks. Its usual food was tea-leaves, tobacco, potato-parings, and porter! When we left England for India, Billy was handed over to our Quartermaster-Sergeant's father, with instructions as to his food. The Y Battery brought home a dromedary, which had been captured during the war; and the P Battery brought home a boar from Kenlow. The men always have a liking for a pet of some sort.

I left Balaklava Harbour on the 6th of June 1856, for England, landing at Woolwich on the 25th of July following. I could have had a month's furlough, but Lieutenant Majendie, of my battery, wanted his groom to go to Scotland for a month first, so I was content with only a week, as I only had five pounds to spend.

I had been away from England more than two years, and was looking forward to a spell at home, but fate decreed otherwise; and in less than twelve months we were ordered to embark for India to assist in quelling the Mutiny.

After a voyage of four months we arrived at Calcutta, and took our guns to Dum-Dum, where we left them in the Riding School; and then returned to Calcutta, crossed the Ganges in boats, and took train to Raneegunge, where we were served out with carbines, and started to march to Cawnpore by the Grand Trunk Road.

On our arrival we were told the following tale of suffering and misery: -- Major-General Sir H. M. Wheeler, K.C.B., who was in command of the troops there, upon hearing the reports of' the mutiny, set his men to work to make an intrenchment. The task was a most tedious one and slow of progress, for labour was scarce and the soil was almost as hard as rock. That which was thrown up to form a parapet was not moistened and beaten down, in consequence of the scarcity of water, so that the crest of the mound was not even bullet-proof. Two nine-pounders and six field guns were all that were taken into the intrenchment, and a quantity of ammunition was, for security, buried under ground. No very elaborate arrangements for feeding seemed to have been made.

The number of those who took refuge in the enclosure was

four hundred and fifty-five men, two hundred and twenty-five women, and three hundred and twenty children, besides a few native servants and officers who were allowed to take shelter with them.

The native troops soon surrounded the intrenchment, keeping up a murderous fire with two eighteen-pounders and about half a dozen smaller guns. The two barrack buildings, around which the trench had been dug, were soon reduced to ruins, so that some of the poor souls had to huddle together in the innermost rooms, where now and then a shell would burst, killing large numbers of them; while others crept into holes dug out near the embankment, and covered with floor boards taken from the ruins, to shelter them from the sun's rays.

The water for the whole of the people had to be drawn from an unprotected well in the centre of the intrenched position. The mutineers kept up a continual fire whenever they saw anyone go near it, and many lost their lives in endeavouring to procure water for their suffering wives and little ones.

There was another well a little distance from the intrenchment, and in the silent night, under cover of the darkness, those who had been killed during the day were carried and reverently lowered into it.

On the night of the second day of the siege a party of Englishmen bravely made a sortie, and, after a severe hand-to-hand struggle, succeeding in spiking three small guns and one large one; but their efforts were fruitless, for the rebels brought from the magazine, which unfortunately had not been destroyed, two nine-pounders, two eighteen-pounders, five twenty-four pounders, and four mortars. Each gun used to throw between twenty and thirty shots an hour; and, in addition to this terrible fire, between five and six thousand mutineers kept up such a storm of bullets, that men, women, children, and babies in arms were killed; and nothing could surpass the awful miseries and

horrible privations of the besieged garrison. Many died from exposure, others entirely lost their reason through the terrible heat, the thermometer ranging from one hundred and twenty to one hundred and thirty degrees.

The mutineers were commanded by an important personage among them, called Nana Sahib, who, finding after a siege of eighteen days that he could not get the better of the plucky Englishmen, sent an Englishwoman, whom he had taken prisoner, with a written proposition to the General, that if they would lay down their arms they should receive a safe passage to Allahabad, promising to provide carriages for the women and children, and covered boats to convey them all down the river.

General Wheeler afterwards had a conference with some natives, sent by Nana Sahib, at which it was stipulated that the English should march out under arms, with sixty rounds of ammunition per man. An agreement was drawn up and signed by the General, and then taken to Nana, who returned it duly signed, and ratified by a solemn oath.

Accordingly, early in the morning of Saturday the 27th of June, a number of vehicles arrived at the intrenchment, and the evacuation commenced about 6 a.m. The noble little band consisted of only four hundred and fifty all told, and they proceeded to the river, where they found the boats, but nearly every one of them was aground. The officers and men walked into the shallow water, and with great difficulty got them afloat, and helped the wounded and the women and children into them, while a vast crowd of natives stood upon the bank watching the embarkation.

Unfortunately the dry season had, as usual, caused the river to be at its lowest, and suddenly, before the first boat had fairly started, a bugle was blown as a signal, and a number of guns concealed on both sides of the river were instantly discharged at the heavily-laden boats, in addition to a storm of grape and musketry.

A number of native troopers then entered the water and massacred all the men who were still alive, except four, who, after marvellous adventures, escaped by swimming down the stream.

The poor women and children were then brought out of the river; many of the little ones were forcibly taken from their mothers' arms by the inhuman troopers, tossed into the air, and caught upon swords, bayonets, and spear-points; while others were torn limb from limb, and their tiny bodies cast into the river. The survivors, Numbering about one hundred and twenty, were then marched four miles under a July sun, many of them with bare feet, having lost their shoes in the water, and, having at length arrived at Nana's camp, they were thrust into a large room with other English prisoners who had been captured in the city.

When news reached Nana that the British troops were approaching, that they were within twenty miles, that there was no resisting them, that they were making headway against fearful odds, like mad horses or mad dogs, caring neither for cannon nor musketry, a conference was held, at which it was suggested that it was the thought of the women and children in captivity which urged the British on, but that if they were slaughtered, the Europeans, being only a handful in number, would be discouraged and go back.

It was thereupon agreed that the prisoners should be put to death, and a few men -- some say five, some seven -- entered the building in which the prisoners were confined, about six in the evening, under the command of a woman named Hosainee Khanum, or the Begum, who had the superintendence of the prisoners, and then commenced one of the most barbarous butcheries on record. This continued till dark, when the doors of the building were closed for the night.

On the following morning the doors were again opened, and some three or four ladies and two or three children were found still alive. Some natives, who had been told off for the duty, brought out the dead and threw them into a well close by; and, in the presence of thousands of spectators, the living, who made an effort to escape, were captured and thrown with the dead into the well.

Meanwhile, at Futtehgurh, the non-military residents had prepared a fleet of boats, and on the evening of the 3rd of June, receiving information that a party of insurgents were approaching, and fearing the 10th Regiment of Native Infantry stationed in the town would join them, they embarked on board the boats and started up the river to Cawnpore. Upon approaching the city they found it in the hands of the rebels. Their progress also was arrested by some sand-banks, and a party of mutineers waded into the water to capture them. Some escaping, fled for shelter into the long grass which grew upon the river's bank, but this was set on fire, and they perished miserably. The rest of the captives were bound with ropes and driven to Nana's camp; and there, in the presence of Bala, his brother, the party was fired upon, and those who were not then killed were slaughtered with swords and bayonets. The poor mangled bodies were then stripped, loaded upon carts, and thrown into the Ganges.

Nana, knowing that we had arrived within easy distance of Cawnpore, blew up the magazine, and fled from the city with a company of cut-throats numbering about five thousand.

All this terrible story of cowardice and inhuman cruelty, told us by an Englishman disguised as a native, added to the sight of the ruined intrenchment of General Wheeler, the wells containing the bodies of the dead, and the house in which the massacre of women and children took place, filled us with a burning desire for revenge. Without any unnecessary delay, but waiting only long enough for Sir Colin Campbell to make the necessary arrangements, we crossed the Ganges by the bridge of boats, and started for the relief of Lucknow.

Brigadier-General Hope Grant had previously marched his column of about five thousand men from Cawnpore to Alumbagh, where he joined the small force left in charge of Havelock's baggage, and waited the arrival of Sir Colin Campbell.

We reached Alumbagh without many adventures; and then our work began in earnest, for we had to fight our way into the heart of the town.

I well remember a Sepoy who, while we were halting, kept up a continual fire upon us, till Captain Gibbon said to a sergeant of the Rifles, "Can't you get that man out of that?" The sergeant said he would try, and sighting his rifle at nine hundred yards, he rested it on the wheel of the gun and waited. Presently the man came out from behind a tree, and was about to fire again, when the sergeant let fly, and we saw the man throw up his arms, leap into the air, and fall like lead.

When we began to storm the town, an old Hindoo, who stood on top of one of the flat-roofed houses, bowed to us most ceremoniously, I suppose to show us he was friendly; but our orders were to fire, and fire we did, our Captain saying, with a laugh, "I can't help it, old chap," and down he went with the ruins.

On the racecourse the mutineers had taken up a position in the grand stand, and kept up a continual fire upon our infantry. My battery was directing its fire on the town, when an infantry officer came up and said to our officer, "I wish you would come and put a round or two into that grand stand." He replied, "I dare not leave my position without orders, but I will come as soon as possible." Some time afterwards we went towards the grand stand, and fired three rounds into it, and the enemy fled.

A young officer, whom I did not know, drew his sword and went forward to enter the building, but a wretched Sepoy, who was hiding behind the door, fired and killed him. I shall never forget the rage the men were in, and the punishment they meted out to the fellow.

Amongst the prisoners we captured here were two native generals, and, without giving them any trial, we hung them in a garden.

I was giving our horses water at the river, when a round shot came plump in front of the horse I was riding, giving him such a start backwards that I was pitched clean over his head into the water. This raised a laugh at my expense, but it was near enough for me.

While we were awaiting instructions, two of our drivers went off looting, which was against orders. They marched into a house not far from us, and there they found a woman in bed guarding some valuables with a drawn sword. They pulled her out with very little ceremony, and having taken the sword from her, took the jewels also, and left her all distressed. They brought two prisoners back with them as a sort of peace-offering, and these were hanged soon afterwards.

We entered the town by the iron bridge. Sir Colin Campbell entered from the college, and captured a nine-pounder, which had been giving us a lot of trouble. I shall never forget the fight at that iron bridge. As we drove the rebels across it into the town, they fled from it by the stone bridge, about fourteen hundred yards distant, and got away in our rear; but not without severe loss, for our guns were pointed at the stone bridge, and we killed large numbers of them as they endeavoured to escape.

A comrade near me had a narrow escape; a piece of shell carried his haversack from his side without wounding him. Another comrade had his beard shot away; while a third had a bullet through his turban.

After the capture of the town, we rested a day or two in a palace, during which time we had several opportunities of looting.

I got a few rings, but had to limit myself to insignificant articles, as I had nowhere to put anything. In fact, men who had loaded themselves up had to throw their treasures away in consequence of the fatigue. I went into a native jeweller's workshop, where I found a chest of small drawers filled with precious stones, and couldn't help myself.

We were ordered to form a flying column, and started at the signal of three guns, but on arriving at Donnybridge found the rebels had been drawn from their position and defeated by the 27th Madras Native Infantry. We went out for eight miles, but finding the country deserted, we returned to camp; and the following morning we left the road and cut our way through the jungle towards Cawnpore; and a terrible march it was.

I remember on the 12th of May we lost several men with sunstroke, and I heard General Hope Grant say it was the hottest day he had ever seen. Captain Gibbons was in command of our artillery, and Captain Johnson in command of my battery, and we had a thousand native cavalry to cover our guns. We came upon a swarm of mutineers, who surrounded us and killed the best part of our grass-cutters, but we drove them across the salt-pans; and, darkness coming on, we retired a few yards, and having posted pickets, lay down for the night beside our guns, the horses being still hooked on.

In the middle of the night a picket of 7th Hussars raised a false alarm, having heard the enemy retreating through the jungle. We had a few casualties in the darkness, for we couldn't tell blacks from whites. Captain Gibbons was just getting out of his dooly, when a friendly black knocked him down by mistake, and the fall fired his revolver, which lodged a bullet in his leg and rendered him useless.

Finding the country quiet, we returned to Lucknow. A day or two after, seeing the enemy at a considerable distance, we set out to march towards them under cover of the darkness. About four in the morning our advance guard came upon a crowd of rebels, one of whom called out, "Who goes there?" and one of our natives answered, "Europeans"; whereupon, bang went a gun, and a portion of a shell struck our ammunition waggon, but fortunately did no damage. We turned eighteen field guns upon them, and soon put them into confusion.

In front of where I was, the second and third battalions of Rifles charged about two thousand of their dismounted cavalry, and this prevented our cavalry from charging them, and my battery from firing, for a while. However, after some hard fighting, we set them in motion, and had the satisfaction of utterly routing them. Our officers estimated their number at sixty thousand; and Nina Sahib was believed to have been amongst them, but well in the rear.

Next day we were paraded to witness the presentation of the Victoria Cross to a private of the Rifle Brigade, for having killed three mutineers with a short sword, and rescued a comrade while himself severely wounded.

A little while after this we had to march for sixty miles while the monsoons were raging, and this was a work of great difficulty, but there was no fighting then; and soon afterwards the natives began to come into camp and lay clown their arms. After taking everything from them, we let them go, except any that were proved to have been concerned in the massacre at Cawnpore, and these we killed either by hanging or blowing them from the guns.

On peace being restored, we marched to Dum-Dum, where I remained till some time in 1860, when I returned to England; and in 1864 embarked for South Africa, under Captain Mall, and remained at King William's Town till 1869, when we proceeded to Mauritius; and at the latter end of 1871 embarked for St. Helena, where I remained about two years.

I took my discharge at Woolwich in January 1874, after a

service of twenty-one years, five months, and six clays, wearing the Crimean medal with three clasps, the Turkish medal, the Mutiny medal with clasp for assisting in the capture of Lucknow, and a Good Conduct medal, and being entitled to a pension of a shilling a day.

Tommy Atkins' War Stories: 9

Rough Work in the Crimea

By Sergeant-Major Richard Ellis

3rd Regiment of Foot

Ellis served with both the 57th Middlesex
Regiment and the 21st Royal North
British Fusiliers and relates his experiences
in India before reaching the Crimea.

Rough Work in the Crimea

I joined the 57th Middlesex Regiment at the age of eighteen, at Inniscorthy, County Wexford, on the 20th January 1841. On the 7th March of the same year I embarked with the draft on board the troopship *General Kidd*, and landed at Madras on 2nd July.

For four years and five months we saw but little change, except the ordinary drills and various marches, till on the 30th November 1845 the regiment marched to Arnee to be disbanded, and volunteers were called for to join other regiments.

I chose the 21st Royal North British Fusiliers, joining them on the 1st December following; and soon afterwards the order came to proceed by forced marches to the North-Western Provinces. On the march we were stopped, and sent to Agra, as Sobraon had fallen. We afterwards left Agra and marched to Cawnpore, where we remained for about a year and nine months; when we were ordered to proceed to Calcutta, and embark for England on the 14th January 1848.

During my eight years in India I saw many marvellous sights, so many, indeed, that I can scarcely set my mind on any particular one to begin with.

Here goes for the Fakirs. I remember once seeing one seated on his haunches by the roadside, in front of a charcoal fire, roasting his knees by way of penance. When I say roasting I mean actually burning, -- the flesh was peeling from his bones and frizzling, while the fat dropped on to the fire and added to the intense heat. All the while the man sat without moving a muscle, as though he were at his ease. Our Colonel remarked, as we passed, "What a foolish man!" but he took no heed of us.

Once, at Arnee, I was out for a walk with a comrade, when presently we noticed a large toad blown out to an enormous size, and getting a little nearer to inspect it, we found ourselves face to face with a cobra, which was just going to swallow the toad. On seeing us he raised himself about three feet, and in another moment would have darted upon us, but we beat a retreat, and called to some natives who were working in an adjoining plantation. They ran to us with long bamboos, and beat the snake to death. Thereupon we fastened our prize to one of the bamboos, and brought it to barracks. It measured five feet eight inches and a half.

I remember, when at Burdwan, visiting the King's Menagerie, by permission of His Majesty, who sent his bodyguard to escort us round. Here we saw large numbers of alligators kept in tanks, besides large numbers of animals of every description.

I saw, after the battle of Sobraon, when the captured guns were marched down by the 62nd Regiment, our cannons had been so accurately aimed that several balls were lodged in the muzzles of the enemy's guns.

I had also the pleasure of seeing Pungent-Singh, the King of Cabul, who had been the cause of the war, brought down prisoner. The King of Bhurtpore watched his arrival, and I saw him seated on his horse, with a most magnificent display of jewels on his trappings, weeping at the sight of the guns being brought and placed in line in the park outside Agra.

I saw, on the banks of the Jumna, at the back of Allahabad, large numbers of native pilgrims from all parts of the country getting water in large leather bottles, which they carried away on payment of a fee to a priest in charge. This water would afterwards be sold, when brought home, at enormous prices.

A gigantic idol, carved in stone, was placed upon the river

bank, and painted with red ochre, and this the natives worshipped. At Cawnpore I witnessed a native festival called Ramma Luchman, where an enormous figure of this god with seven heads -- who is believed by the Hindoos to drink up the Ganges -- was filled with combustibles, and the fire flamed from his seven mouths, to impress the populace, who were there in large numbers. Nana Sahib stood near where I was enjoying the amusement. He had robbed his brother, the King of Oude, of two lakhs of rupees, and had placed himself under the protection of the East India Company at Cawnpore. He drove out daily for exercise in an open carriage, and we saw him very often. He was a determined-looking man, and appeared to be capable of doing all the devilment of which he afterwards was guilty.

Nautch girls I have seen in plenty, dancing to the music of the tom-tom, played by men who go about the country with them and act as their protectors and keepers, just as we may imagine a theatrical company would do out there. Snake-charming never had much interest for me, and I seldom took the trouble to look on at a performance. Juggling was more to my fancy, and I have seen some very wonderful performances by the men who devote their time to it.

At last the time came for me to leave India, and after a voyage round the Cape in the *Monarch*, one of Green's merchantmen, my regiment reached England, and was quartered at the Infantry Barracks in Canterbury, with the 50th and the 28th, which had returned at the same time.

In consequence of so much money having been saved by the men abroad, it was here spent pretty freely, and naturally brought on free fights; and our regiment, which was perhaps the worst, was ordered to proceed forthwith to Edinburgh.

On the 6th of July 1848, I was promoted corporal, an appointment I might have had years before if I had not preferred my liberty; and on the 14th of the following month I was made a sergeant. I celebrated this event by marriage nine days afterwards. For five years I was quartered at various places in Scotland, till, on the 27th October 1853, when the regiment was stationed in Dublin, I was promoted to the rank of colour-sergeant.

At this time England was preparing for the Russian War, and our regiment was one of the first to receive orders to get in readiness, and make the regiment up to one thousand two hundred strong. This was accomplished by taking volunteers from other regiments. All was excitement when we started by train for Cork, where we awaited the arrival of the *Golden Fleece*, which was to take us to the Crimea.

We had a pleasant voyage out, many ships going with us. They formed into four lines, at a distance apart of a few cable lengths, when we reached Balchic Bay. We disembarked at Eupatoria about the 16th of September, and a very unfortunate disembarkation it was. One of the heaviest night rains that ever fell drenched us through and through. I was with my company on the outlying picket, and shall never forget my experience. We had no shelter from the storm but greatcoats and blankets. It was impossible to lie down, and the whole of the men kept moving about on the miserable beach to keep themselves alive and warm. No lights or watch-fires were possible. Officers and men shared alike the misery, which seemed unending. We welcomed the first streak of daylight, and when the sun rose the rain ceased; but by this time many of our men were groaning with cholera, and had to be re-embarked. Not one of my own company that did so have I seen since.

The next two days were occupied in unloading stores, guns, and ammunition, and loading waggons. The French fleet, which was engaged in the same work a little farther off, had better appliances for the purpose, and we were annoyed by seeing them ready to march long before we were.

At Old Fort, Eupatoria, we drained dry the only well we could find, but were not allowed to forage. A fine field of onions tempted us sorely. We dared not disobey the standing order of the army, although the French cleared the country for miles round of sheep, cows, bullocks, and everything eatable they could find.

They had to bring their spoil past our lines, and the sheep becoming wild at the sight of the tents which we had been able to pitch, ran in all directions. One accidentally got into my tent, where my store-man and his brother were busy cleaning up, and that lost sheep never went out again, for, having killed it, we dug a hole inside the tent and buried the offal, and covered the place with a blanket. We divided the carcase amongst the company; and presently a Frenchman complained to Lord Raglan, who sent one of his staff with an interpreter to make inquiries. But as we were unable to give him any information on the subject, the matter dropped, and we enjoyed our supper.

About this time I was afraid I was stricken with the cholera, but the kind attention which I received at the hands of my friends in the company, which I shall never forget, brought me round.

After about three days' marching, we arrived at a large mansion, which was said to be Prince Gortschakoff's country seat. The place was deserted, and the men in advance of us had made havoc of everything they found there, smashing all the furniture and the windows, and completely destroying the place. We found some splendid apples in the orchard, with which we filled our haversacks.

We proceeded to bivouac in a small wood near here, and guards, outlying pickets, and sentries were posted, arms piled, and most of the men asleep in the open air under their blankets and greatcoats, when a baggage mule broke loose, and, taking fright, ran helter-skelter through the wood. Many men started to their feet, crying out, "The enemy is on us!" and in a moment the whole of the division was rushing about in the darkness, groping for their arms; such a panic I had never before seen. By the time the mistake was found out, and everything got into order again, it was nearly time to march.

On the following day we came in sight of the barricades erected by the Russians, on the hills overlooking the plain, across which our troops were advancing. About midday, bang! went the first gun. "Hullo, boys!" I cried, "now we are at it, it won't be long before we are into it." Then came more heavy firing, ploughing up the ground around us, scattering dust all over us, and sweeping many of our men down like ninepins.

Lord Cathcart, one of the finest officers I have ever seen, called out, "Be cool, men, in your formations"; and after a while the whole of the regiments were formed in fighting line, some of them going into action while others were forming up.

It was terrible work this forming up under fire; many of our men were spattered with the brains and blood of their comrades, to whom they had been speaking but a short time before. Every man who fell had to be left on the ground until assistance came to him; no man was allowed to assist a wounded comrade, his own services being required at the front. As the gaps occurred, the men closed up, and with as little delay as possible the order was given to charge.

To get at the heights, we had to drive out long lines of sharp-shooters, who were in position, and doing much execution. These men held the ground as long as they were able, but eventually had to beat a retreat across the shallow river, and we went after them with fixed bayonets.

We were told later on that the Russians had expected to hold their position for six weeks against any force that could be brought against them; and we saw many ladies (who had come to view the destruction of our forces) moving about among the

Russians, but when our field guns opened fire they soon retired. We went up the heights with a rush and a cheer. Indeed, everything throughout the day was done in so great a hurry that we had no time to think of details. I shall never forget the excitement of driving the enemy from their stronghold. When at last they broke, and fled in disorder, our men gave chase and killed large numbers of them. The plain beyond the hills was literally strewn with their dead.

At last the bugle sounded "Cease firing," and we mustered in the place occupied by the Russians in the morning.

The rest of the day was spent in preparing for the night, placing pickets all round the camp, finding comfortable quarters, and cooking our rations, of which we had three days' supply in our haversacks. We found no food belonging to the enemy, -- they had no doubt taken with them all they had. They left their arms and accoutrements on the ground with their dead and wounded. I remember one Pole pointing to the letter "P" on his cap to show that he was not a Russian, and offering me a decoration that hung round his neck if I would give him a drink of water. I gave the poor fellow a drop of rum; he was terribly wounded, having both his legs broken.

That night many of the bandsmen of the regiment's, and others, worked like slaves to bring in the wounded. Those who could not be moved were covered with blankets and left for the night. The surgeons worked untiringly, and did all that human skill could do for English and Russians alike. While one of the doctors was passing round the field among the dying, a wounded Russian took aim at him, and would have fired had not one of our men noticed him and pinned him to the ground with his bayonet.

I was on outlying picket duty with my company, and the moans, yells, groans, and cries of despair, suffering, and agony, were terrible to hear, and had an indescribable effect upon our men.

When the sun rose next morning, we were allowed to wander for a short time about the battlefield, but the strongest heart was soon affected by the awful scenes. Our own men were lying mingled with the enemy one on top of another, many of them clutching at each other in their death agony. As they had fallen, so they lay; many had writhed about during the night in terrible suffering, and we saw such sights that several of the men in my company fainted with sheer horror and repulsion. One friend of mine in particular suffered terribly.

The pioneers of all the regiments were set to work to dig long trenches about seven feet wide for the interment of the dead. Men were sent out in all directions to collect the bodies, which were brought up on stretchers, and laid, like sardines in a box, in about three layers, as near as I can remember, and then the earth was filled in and a large mound made over them. Our dead were buried by themselves, but no volleys were fired over them; and I saw no chaplain in the Crimea till near the close of the war, although several were there.

The work of burying the dead, and collecting the arms, occupied two days. Every man who was not wanted for other duty was ordered to assist; and they made a good collection of money from the dead, for it did no one good to bury it. I saw several cases of mutilation of the dead, particularly of a colour-sergeant of the 57th, whose finger was cut off for the sake of his ring.

As there was no pay issued during the first part of the campaign, the military chests of the regiments being on board the ships, the money taken from the dead all went into the canteens for drink, the French taking most of it. The commonest drink obtained from the French was a certain powerful spirit, and being drunk by men who had very little food to eat, it often brought on dysentery.

When I saw men in my company attacked, I often said, "I must send you to the hospital"; and they would answer, "Let me remain where I am, I might as well die here as there." And I can safely say I lost through sickness more men of my company, which was the strongest in the regiment, than from actual fighting.

When all the dead were buried, and the wounded and prisoners sent on board ship, the order was given to march. This was on the 23rd September. We had no adventures till we took up our position on the heights, three miles from Sebastopol.

A Russian ship, called the *Twelve Apostles*, which was lying in the harbour of Sebastopol, soon caused us uneasiness by firing several enormous shots into our camp. We retired about a mile, and rested on the ever-memorable ground now called Cathcart's Hill, from the fact that General Cathcart, who commanded our division, was buried there. Our division comprised the Rifle Brigade, the 17th, 20th, 21st, 46th, 48th, 57th, 63rd, and 68th Regiments.

Having settled down out of range of the guns, our heavy task of making the trenches and erecting the Green Hill twenty-one gun battery commenced.

The Engineers laid out the ground for the zigzags, as we called them, and the men worked continuously every night, under cover of the darkness and by the aid of dark lanterns, until the trenches and batteries extended in front of the Green Hill battery, which faced the Redan.

Our ships had landed twenty-one sixty-eight pounders at Balaklava, and these were brought up by the sailors and marines, who sang at their work, although it was great labour to get the guns into position in the Green Hill battery. Afterwards five other guns were placed in the five-gun battery.

We lost a good many men during this work, for they were exposed to the enemy's fire most of the time.

On the 5th of November, which was Sunday, after returning from digging in the trenches, my regiment was preparing for a short rest, when the bugles sounded the "Assembly," and we were under arms at once, as there was a cry that the enemy were in our camp. Without waiting to take off overcoats or undo belts, my regiment formed, and moved on with great spirit, notwithstanding the men had been labouring in the trenches all night.

The rain was coming down in torrents, and the fog was very dense, so that we could hardly tell friends from foes. As we hurried forward we met the 77th Regiment , which, having exhausted its supply of ammunition in checking the advance of the enemy, called to us as they fell back for a fresh supply, saying, "Move on 21st, our ammunition is gone." We rushed to the position, took up the firing, and laid it into the enemy volley by volley. I believe that no round was lost, but that every bullet had its billet. This continued for several hours; and we, having plenty of fresh ammunition supplied us, were enabled to hold our ground against large bodies of the enemy until the Algerians, belonging to the French force, came up at the double, and being fresh, and well equipped for the purpose, charged at the enemy, and we with them, prodding with the bayonet every fallen Russian we passed. If they were dead it did them no harm, if they were only wounded it prevented the treachery from which we had suffered more than once.

We rushed on, yelling, and firing with as much accuracy as possible under the great excitement. The Russians gave way in as steady order as though they were on parade. When our ammunition had run out, I ordered the men who had knives to cut the pouches from the dead Russians, and, exchanging rifles, we went after them, firing at them with their own weapons. Shells were bursting over us in all directions, and a splinter struck me on the head and rendered me unconscious.

When I recovered consciousness I found that I had also received a bullet through the muscle of my right arm, and another embedded in my left, leg between the calf and the bone. A bandsman of my company, whom I discovered lying near me slightly wounded in the side, assisted me to the hospital tent, where I found the doctors all busy and the place almost afloat with blood. I was temporarily attended to, and the bullet being extracted from my leg, I was carried to my own tent, where I lay for seven days, getting worse.

On the morning of the 14th came the greatest storm I have ever witnessed. In a moment, without any warning, the tent pole snapped like the stem of a tobacco pipe, and the canvas was carried bodily away. Whatever loose articles were about were blown from the heights down into Sebastopol, and I was left lying on my buffalo robe, which constituted my only bed. Every tent in the regiment, with the exception of Lord West's, was blown down; and the greatest confusion prevailed. The rain and wind combined were terrific, and we had nowhere to take shelter, and to light a fire was impossible. In the evening, when the storm abated a little, the men managed to get the canvas up again, and I was placed in the regimental hospital.

Here it was considered necessary to amputate both my leg and arm, but I strongly protested; and as one of the doctors said that he had treated a similar case without amputation, I was allowed to retain those useful appendages, and gradually became convalescent.

Soon afterwards I resumed my duties in the trenches; and about this time one of the sergeants of my company was charged by the officer, going his rounds, with being asleep at his post. I was ordered to place him under arrest, which I did. He was tried by court-martial, and sentenced "to be shot to death by musketry."

As I knew that he had always been a good and faithful sergeant, and that, even if he had been asleep, he deserved pardon on account of having been continually in the trenches hard at work digging and watching, almost in the teeth of the enemy, and had thus become exhausted, I asked the company if we should memorialise Lord Raglan, through the officer commanding.

The men with one accord said, "Yes, do all you can." So I prepared a petition, and took it round to all the officers, not one of whom declined to sign; and the officer who had given the man in charge signed it also. I handed the document to Lord West, who presented it to Lord Raglan, who soon afterwards came to our company, and I was ordered by Lord West, who was in attendance, to bring the prisoner before them.

Lord Raglan, addressing the prisoner, said, "Sergeant, in consequence of the good conduct of the regiment to which you belong, and the good character you have always borne, I make you a present of your life."

As soon as the men of the regiment heard this speech, they gave three cheers for his lordship that made the hills resound, and must have been heard down in Sebastopol. The sergeant, who was a great favourite, was immediately shouldered back to his tent. We often heard the French shooting in subordinates. They appeared to be more severe than the English.

One morning I was sent for by Lord West, who had just received papers from England, and ordered to find the correspondent of the Times newspaper, and to desire him to strike his tent and leave the camp. I complied with this command, and so did he.

The Russians made many sorties into our trenches, which were repulsed on all occasions, and treated in a very business-like way. The enemy often kept up continual showers of balls, shells, and bullets into our trenches. Larger shells made a peculiar noise, and the sailors who were with us called them "Whistling Dicks."

When the firing slackened, we used to get on with the work of digging, leaving one man to watch the puffs of smoke at the enemy's batteries. He used to call out "Down!" every time he saw one, and we would then crouch down till the shot had passed over us; but very often men were hit, and so the work of death went on. Officers going the round would often find sentries dead at their posts. Sometimes a shell would burst in a trench, knocking out the brains of one, smashing the face of another, cutting off the arm of a third, breaking the back of a fourth, splintering the leg of a fifth, and spreading dismay among us. Then we would take up the dead men, who a moment before had been cheerfully talking to us, and lay them together to await the time when we went off duty. In dead and wounded we used to lose an enormous number of men a month at this fearful work.

On one occasion a shell lodged on the bank and rolled back into our trench, falling close to my feet. A private, named Madigan, who was standing by me, picked it up, pulled out the fuse, and threw the shell over the parapet. I brought this act of courage under the notice of Lord West, and in consequence, Madigan received a medal for distinguished service, which carried with it an annuity of five pounds.

The Russian Emperor called January, February, and March, of 1855, his best generals, because he knew the severity of the weather would do his work; and sure enough it would have done, if we had taken Sebastopol and followed him into the country, but our generals were not such fools, and considered it better to remain near the coast and let the Russians send their forces to Sebastopol to maintain their dignity.

The weather indeed was terribly severe. The trenches were filled over and over again with snow, which had to be cleared out. Many men were frost-bitten, and it was pitiful to see their sufferings. In fact it is impossible to describe the misery endured by our men. The only thing that kept life in us was the drop of rum which was issued to us night and morning. The coffee was served out in green beans, and we had to attempt to roast it in the small fires which we could get now and then. The War Office sent out coffee-mills, which were useless under the circumstances, and made us laugh.

There seemed to be bad luck upon us the whole time. The meat was served out to us raw and salt, and we had no wood to light fires wherewith to cook it. Of bread and flour we had none, and biscuits were in many cases nothing but bags of dust and mildew. Water was scarce, and often we had to use the melted snow.

Boots and clothing were worn out, and there were none to replace them until the Benevolent Fund was started in England, and out came many articles that cheered the hearts of officers and men alike.

At last I began to wear out, and was sent with others to Malta, on board the *Himalaya*. Soon after my arrival I caught the Maltese fever, and the sight of food was loathsome to me. However, I came round at last, and was appointed Sergeant-Major of the 4th Division Provisional Battalion; and on the conclusion of the war, when my regiment came to the island, I reverted once more to the rank of colour-sergeant. On the 31st August 1858, by general orders, I was appointed to the rank of Sergeant-Major in the 3rd Foot, and remained in that regiment till I took my discharge.

During this time my wife and family had been sent out from England by the kindness of Lord West.

I remember, in Malta, a gunner of the foot artillery attempting to shoot the orderly officer of his company, and for this offence he was condemned to be shot. The whole of the men in the garrison were paraded and pontooned across the harbour to Valetta, where the execution was to take place.

The Burial Service was read by the chaplain, and the prisoner was blindfolded by the provost-marshal and conducted to the spot on which he was to suffer, which was strewn with sawdust, the coffin being placed by the man's side. A party of twelve men were served out with rifles, six only being loaded, so that the men could not tell which of them caused the death. The provost-marshal was a gunner, and a friend of the prisoner, and had, by the prisoner's request, been appointed to the post for the day only. He bound the hands of the condemned man behind his back, and placed him in position, with his face to the firing party, and the sea behind him. The man went down on one knee, and the sergeant in command of the firing party gave in an undertone the words, Ready! Present!! Fire!!! The poor fellow fell to the ground riddled with shots, and the troops were ordered to march past, with the command to each company, "Eyes right!" and after that we saw no more of him.

The Czar of Russia came to Malta some short time after the war was concluded, and was entertained by Sir John Pennefather, who was at that time in command of the island. The garrison was paraded in review order, for the inspection of His Majesty, and as he passed down the ranks the General explained that the majority of these were young men sent out from England to fill up the blanks in each regiment. I, being centre sergeant of the colour party, the Emperor, as he passed, stretched out his hand and touched the five medals on my breast, saying, "This is not a young one."

Without many adventures, the time passed pleasantly till I sailed for England; and on the 10th of June 1862 I took my discharge, after serving for twenty-one years and one hundred and forty-three days.

Tommy Atkins' War Stories: 10

In the Maori Rising

By Joseph Hinton

58th Regiment

Joseph Hinton describes his time of action in New Zealand with the Rutland Regiment during the Maori Rising.

In the Maori Rising

The best shilling I ever saw in my life was the one I took at Brompton Barracks, on the 6th of December 1843, when I joined the 58th Foot, Rutland-shire (now Northamptonshire) Regiment.

About six months afterwards my company was ordered to march to Gravesend for service abroad. We embarked on the *Sir Robert Peel*, and went up to Deptford; where we took on board two hundred and fifty convicts, who came to the ship's side in small boats, under the charge of warders, while we formed a guard, each man with his firelock, or "Brown Bess," loaded, to prevent any attempt at escape. The convicts were all handcuffed, and were conducted down into the hold, which had been fitted up with berths for their, accommodation. They were afterwards brought on. deck singly, and one of our men, who had been a blacksmith, had to rivet an iron ring upon each ankle. A long chain, fastened to a belt round the man's waist was fixed to each ring, and these were not taken off till we landed the convicts at Hobart Town, in Tasmania, except in cases of good conduct, when the men were allowed to work on board.

Our time was taken up in watching the prisoners, and we were glad to reach the end of our journey, which occupied five months and a half.

From Hobart Town we proceeded to Sydney, where we embarked on a small steamer, and went up the river to Paramatta, staying for three months, and being joined soon afterwards by a draft of fifty or sixty men.

At this time we heard of disturbances with the natives in New Zealand, and were ordered back to Sydney, and embarked in the sailing brig *Bee*, and after a pretty rapid passage arrived off shore near Wellington. Having got as near the beach as possible in the ship's boats, we waded ashore, and marched at once to a stockade, prepared for us by settlers, upon the banks of the Hutt River.

We were a happy and careless lot of young fellows, and enjoyed the prospect very much. We lighted a large fire inside the stockade, and, having posted sentinels, lay down to sleep. For three days we were engaged in completing the stockade, and when this was accomplished we filled mattresses with straw, and, having blankets to cover us, were more comfortable at night; and here we continued contented enough for about three months. While here, we were joined by the wife and children of our Colour-Sergeant, who had come from Paramatta with a draft of men who were to remain at Wellington.

Hearing that the Maories were getting troublesome a little farther up the country, forty-eight of us were sent there under Lieutenant Shiply. We were stationed in a small .farmstead near a shallow river, some of us sleeping in small outhouses and the rest of us in a barn. We pitched a small picket tent near the river, and I was on sentry-go from three o'clock till five on the morning of the 16th of May 1845. I then went into the barn to sleep for a little while, but had not slept five minutes before I heard a shot. I called out to my companion, "Look out, mate, there they are!" and out we rushed, and found about two hundred and fifty natives fording the river. Some had reached the picket tent, and were firing through it.

We took up a position behind two trees that had been felled near the barn, and fired volleys into them as fast as we could. Our bugler, who on hearing the first shot had sounded the alarm, was set upon by a lot of the blacks, who were armed with tomahawks; others had flintlock muskets, which they had obtained from whalers in exchange for fresh meat and goods.

While we were firing, the wife of a volunteer, who was camping farther up the country, came out from the Colour-Sergeant's hut, and I called to her to go back or she would be killed. She answered, "I'm all right; I suppose you want some more ammunition?" I replied, "We shall very soon." Whereupon she went into the barn, brought out a cask of cartridges, knocked the head off it, and handed the cartridges to the men, who kept up a steady fire until the Maories retreated across the river; but they remained on the opposite bank firing at us until about half-past nine, when they retired into the bush. They had been accompanied by a number of native women, who picked up their dead and wounded warriors and carried them off, so that we could not tell how many they lost in the engagement.

We found the guard tent riddled with shot; within it the men were all dead, and very much hacked about, except one who was unhurt, and who told us he had pretended to be dead, and that, although the natives had lifted up his eyelids and moved his arms, they had not discovered the fraud.

Poor Corporal Dockrill, in charge of the tent, had the top of his head cut off, and it was hanging down the back of his neck. Private Brett was also very much knocked about; and the bugler had three cuts on his right arm, four on his left, three gashes in his forehead, and his mouth cut from ear to ear, and, what's more, they stole his bugle, and we afterwards heard them sounding it in the wood.

Two days afterwards we sewed up our dead in their blankets, and buried them in one large grave.

A reinforcement was sent up from Wellington, and they camped in a potato field, on the opposite side of the river; but as everything had by that time become quiet, we returned to Wellington, and embarked on the *Calliope*, landing at Wanganui on a

Sunday evening. Here we built a stockade, on a hill overlooking the village, and remained for eighteen months, having only two or three skirmishes during the time. We were only fifty-two all told, so that we had to be pretty cautious. Whenever the men were allowed to go into the town, we used to hoist a black flag with a skull and cross-bones, and if we saw the unfriendly natives assembling, we lowered the flag as a signal for our men to return.

One of our men, named Sculthorp, had bought a fowling-piece at Wellington, and often had permission to go into the bush when the coast was clear. Once, when the order was that nobody was to leave the stockade, he asked me to let him out, as I was in charge of the gate, and on my refusing, he went away and got over the breastwork unperceived, and a little while after we heard from a friendly native that he had been killed. We sent out half a dozen of them with a stretcher, and when they returned, and I lifted the blanket that covered him, I was horrified to find that the blacks had cut his tongue out and scooped out his eyes.

One day, a settler, who lived out in the bush not far from our stockade, left his wife and family in his log-house, while he went out with his gun. He had lived there so long without disturbance, that he did not expect to be molested, or he would have taken refuge in the town. His little son found him out and told him that the blacks had killed his wife and three of his children. The poor fellow was almost distracted, and got some friendly natives to take him across the river in a canoe, and he came to us and reported to our commanding officer, who sent out some friendly natives to bring in the dead bodies, and, on their return, they stated they had heard who had done the deed. Several others were told to accompany them, and they soon returned, bringing with them four prisoners, three men and a boy. Some little time was spent in collecting evidence, and then they were tried by court-martial and condemned to be hung. After being sentenced they were kept for three or four weeks, during which time the missionary visited them many times.

The carpenters who belonged to us were set to work to make a scaffold, and I remember they finished it on the day before the execution was to take place, it being fitted with a crossbeam, a drop, a bolt, and all other necessaries. My old comrade, Shipley, was told off as executioner, and we were formed up into a hollow square to witness the execution. The friendly natives crowded round to see the sight, and the enemy were on the hills on the other side of the river in good numbers. We carried our loaded muskets, and the gun in the stockade was loaded with canister.

The missionary accompanied the men on to the scaffold, and Shipley pinioned their arms and legs and placed white cloths over their eyes. When the commanding officer gave the signal, Shipley came down the steps and drew the bolt, and the three men went down together.

There was a lot of shouting from the enemy on the hills, and they sent in a few men with a white flag to ask for the bodies, but this was refused, and they were all buried in one grave just outside the stockade. The boy was sent on board a Government brig, with orders to the captain not to allow him to land anywhere for, I think it was, seven years. We heard afterwards that he behaved so well that at the end of three years he was released, and went as servant to a naval officer.

Early in the morning of the day following the execution, we were surprised to find the natives had erected a flagstaff on a hill about a thousand yards from us; and our officer told one of the artillerymen, who was a wonderfully good marksman, to take careful aim at it and knock it over, which he did. Soon afterwards we saw it go up again, and the same man brought it down again with another shot. A third time it went up, and a third time it was brought down.

Soon afterwards we saw a native moving about among some flax, that grew in a swamp at some considerable distance from us, watching our movements. Our gunner was ordered to pick him off, and some friendly natives on the following day found the man completely cut in halves.

The enemy had been noticed moving about on the hills near their flagstaff, and presently we saw some of them crossing the river in a canoe. Our commanding officer said to the artillery-man, "Have them out of that!" and I saw the canoe go down with all on board directly after the gun was fired. The others took the precaution to cross farther down the river, where we could not see them, but our scouts told us of it, and we went out to meet them in skirmishing order, taking our field gun with us; but they came on us in such numbers, and with such determination, that our gunners fell back, and left the gun in their possession. We made a rush for it, however, and recovered it in less than four minutes, and at the same time compelled the enemy to retire.

I remember, after the skirmish, seeing one of the artillery propped up on a table having his leg amputated. He had a rum-bottle by his side to give him courage, and during the whole operation he did not say so much as "Oh."

After this matters became quiet, and we went up to Auckland, where they had had some pretty severe fighting; but three months later on I returned to England, and, with others, joined the 4th Company Depot, at Chatham, on December 16th, 1850.

We were sent afterwards to several stations in England; and I married in 1852; and for some time after that we were stationed in Jersey. At that time I was a pioneer corporal, and every other night I had to sit up to turn the gas out in the barracks. I had been seriously thinking over my ignorance, and one evening I said to my wife, who was living in the barracks with me, "My dear, I'm going to teach myself to read and write." She said, "You'll never learn at your time of life." "Won't I?" says I. "I will; and, what's more, I'll teach you too." So next morning I went into the town and bought a few schoolbooks, and we stuck to it till I was made lance-sergeant. We were in Jersey two years, and one day I met the Adjutant in the barrack square, and he called me to him, and having inspected my orderly book, complimented me on it, and soon after I was made sergeant.

On the 4th of January 1865, I took my discharge, having served twenty-one years and twenty-nine days.

Facing the Zulus

By Harry O'Clery

Buffs, East Kent Regiment

O'Clery was present at the outbreak of hostilities and during the siege and relief of Ekowe - now better known as Eshowe - during the Zulu Wars.

Facing the
Zulus

It was at Canterbury, in July 1877, that I joined Her Majesty's forces. I was led to that step by Recruiting-Sergeant Jack Gavigan, who had the credit, while stationed at St. George's Barracks, of enlisting more men in one year than all the other recruiting-sergeants put together.

I was placed in the Depot M Company of the Buffs.

Having received a fairly good education, I soon afterwards sat for an examination, and having gained a second-class certificate, -- which was thought something of in those days, for men were not then up to the present standard of knowledge, -- I was appointed an assistant schoolmaster to the depot, with the remuneration of fourpence a day. It was my duty to take the two lower classes of the men; and I very frequently found myself in charge of the whole school, as the acting schoolmaster, a sergeant whose name I will not disclose, had frequently to repair to the mess for the purpose of refreshment.

About five months after enlisting, I learned that we were ordered to join the regiment at Pietermaritzburg; and soon afterwards we proceeded to Southampton, where we embarked on the ship *American*, and found ourselves in company with a detachment of the 87th Regiment, known as "The Old Fogs," or the "Faugh-a-Ballagh Boys," from the war-cry of the corps; "Fag-an-Bealoch" meaning "Clear the way."

During the voyage to the Cape we heard this war-cry on several occasions, and the monotony of the voyage was varied by occasional fights between men of the two regiments, who probably considered that, as they were going out to fight, there could be no objection to a little practice beforehand; and I can speak from experience in saying that most of my countrymen enjoy nothing better than a lively argument, and a free fight to wind up with.

We encountered a gale off Cape Finisterre, and had to be battened down below; but at this time I was afflicted with sea-sickness, from which I did not recover for seven days. The rest of the voyage was most pleasant and enjoyable.

We disembarked at Cape Town, and after a few days sailed from thence to East London, where we remained about a week, and then proceeded to Durban on *H.M.S. Himalaya.* Owing to the roll of the sea here, we had to land in surf boats. It was anything but a pleasant experience.

Fifteen or twenty men would go down the ship's side into the boat, and a canvas would be stretched over her to keep out the water. Then, in the dark, we found ourselves jerked and jolted, one against another, for some considerable time, until the boat was hauled to the beach, where we landed more dead than alive, for the rolling and pitching of a whole sea voyage was crammed into that brief trip in a surf boat.

After a short stay at Durban, we marched up the country to Pieterniaritzburg, a distance of upwards of fifty miles, which we accomplished in four days, being cheered towards our journey's end by meeting the band of the regiment, which played us into the town to the tune of a then popular comic song. On joining the regiment I was drafted into the B Company.

While staying in the town we turned out to welcome the 24th Regiment, passing through on their way up the country. They stayed about a week, and I made the acquaintance of two brothers, Fred and George Conboy, both in the band.

Soon we learned that Cetewayo, the Zulu King, had been called upon to pay a fine of a certain number of bullocks, for some filibustering expedition which some of his young warriors had made into Natal; and the date of payment was fixed for the 12th January, which was about twelve months after we had left England.

On and before that particular day we were encamped upon the southern bank of the Tugela River, upon which the Royal Engineers, assisted by the soldiers told off for the work, were busily constructing a floating raft, or bridge, by the aid of which we were, if needful, to cross over into the enemy's country.

We numbered in the camp between two and three thousand men, consisting of the Buffs, the 99th Regiment, Mounted Infantry, Naval Brigade, Royal Artillery, a native contingent, and some mounted volunteers from Stanger and Victoria -- two small towns on the coast of Natal -- who evidently thought they were out for a picnic, and brought with them several waggon-loads of bedding, tinned meats, comforts and luxuries, of which I shall say a word or two in the course of my yarn.

The river was very full, and some half a mile wide, and there were plenty of crocodiles in its waters. Two or three poor fellows, while at work on the raft, were snapped up on falling overboard, and seen no more. One was a friend of mine belonging to *H.M.S. Active.*

It was the day before the final pay-day, and away in the distance we could plainly see a body of natives, who were by many in the camp believed to be the people whose arrival we were awaiting. But the commanding officers, I suppose, thought differently, and sent a shell bursting among them to tell them we were there.

The next day we crossed the river, and then war began. The crossing of the river was accomplished this way -- two companies, of about one hundred men each, marched on to the raft, and it was then hauled across by the Naval Brigade. As soon as the men landed on the opposite side, the empty raft was drawn back again for a fresh freight; and so, as it was a tedious job, the whole day was taken up.

From what I could learn of the plan, the British force was to invade the country in four columns. No. 1, nearest the sea, was under the command of Brigadier-General Pearson, numbered 4200, and was to advance along the coast. No. 2 consisted of 3000 natives, commanded by European officers under Colonel Durnford, R.E., who was to cross the Tugela at Middle Drift and march up the left side of the river to Rorke's Drift. No. 3, commanded by Colonel Glyn, was about 3000 strong, and contained the first and second battalions of the 24th Regiment, numbering about 1000 bayonets. And No. 4, under Colonel Evelyn Wood, also about 3000 strong, was to operate from Utrecht, in conjunction with Colonel Glyn's column.

We, in No. 1 column, learned now and then of the movements of the others, by the native runners, who were sent from one column to another with despatches. Poor chaps, they risked their lives for very slight remuneration, and it was dangerous work to play the spy as they did; for the Zulus, when it became known that we were marching on their capital, determined to make a stand for it.

We were marched up country, and terribly wet weather it was, no mistake, for the first week or so. Not a single shot was fired by any of our skirmishers, who were on in front of us. The natives retired before us, keeping, as they went, a watchful eye upon our movements, but taking care to keep out of range. As a proof of their nearness, however, we found, upon coming to their camping-grounds, that the embers of their fires were still smouldering.

Every night we camped in laager. This consists of drawing

the waggons into a circle and digging a slight trench all round it, the earth taken from the trench being thrown up on the outer side to form a breastwork.

Our first laager was formed near the farm of an English settler named John Dunne, who had, I think, married a native woman, and suited himself to the customs of the country. He knew his way about the country, and some little while before we crossed the Tugela he joined our column, bringing with him his family and a large number of followers.

Another stopping-place was upon the banks of a river, and after that at another river. Crossing this at a shallow part, we continued our march, and noticed that traces of the enemy were becoming more and more frequent. This gave us hope of a brush with them.

We were halted to prepare breakfast at a place called Inyezane, when we heard firing in front, and found that our skirmishers were engaged with a Zulu "impi." On pushing forward to the brow of a hill, we found ourselves under fire. Puffs of smoke were appearing in all directions from the bush away in front of us, and we therefore lay down, and fired at every spot from which a puff appeared.

It was my first appearance on a battlefield. We were told by our officers to keep ourselves cool and steady, and fire low; and I tried not to get carried away by the excitement, but it's not so easy, when you know that each puff may mean a dose of death to you or the man next you.

We had with us a naval brigade of two hundred and seventy bluejackets and marines from the *Tenedos* and *Active*, and these had charge of the waggons and two Gatlings. The Zulus came on in fine style, but the steady fire we kept up prevented them coming to close quarters. They, however, attempted a flanking movement; but Colonel Panell led a spirited charge, and cleared the heights, and the enemy were driven off, leaving about nine hundred killed and wounded upon the battlefield. I think we lost in the action seven killed, and about twenty-seven wounded. These we took with us, but left the enemy where they fell.

We had had no breakfast before the fight, and as we had to reach a certain distance each day, we had no refreshment till 9 p.m.

Next day we were overtaken by a native runner, who was taken to the General, and in consequence of the news he brought we were hurried forward with as little delay as possible. These runners are strange individuals; they take to running when they are tired of walking, and I noticed they seemed to get their breath better by so doing.

On the following morning, eleven days after the invasion of the country, we arrived at the village of Ekowe, about forty miles due north of the river Tugela, where there was a mission-station; and here we set to work to build a fort around the church, which was intended to be used as an hospital if required.

We formed a laager, into which we went for safety during the night, the day being occupied in building a fort. Here, upon its completion, we took up our position.

This was how we built the fort. The church tower in the centre was a look-out post for our best marksmen; and around the church, at a considerable distance, we dug a trench, some ten or twelve feet deep, and about twenty feet wide, and into this trench we planted stakes pointed at both ends. The earth from the trench formed a high breastwork, with steps formed on the inner side of the fort; and outside, beyond the trench, we dug small holes, at regular distances apart, into which we drove sharpened stakes, upon which we stretched wire to entangle the legs of the enemy who might venture within the maze.

Our position being considered very secure, the native contingent, with the mounted volunteer picnic-party, were, to the surprise of many of us, sent back, as they could be of no service and would make a considerable difference in our commissariat department.

The mystery of the runner's message was soon cleared up. It turned out that he was the bearer of bad news. A British force had been attacked in camp at Isandlwhana, and literally cut to pieces. In confirmation of the terrible message we happened to capture about this time a Zulu soldier, belonging to the Kandampemvu Regiment, who was wearing a jacket and carrying a rifle which had belonged to a man of the 24th Regiment.

We questioned him about the battle, and the account he gave was that the soldiers and volunteers retired, fighting all the way, and as they got into the camp the Zulus intermingled with them. One party of soldiers came out from among the tents, and formed up a little above the waggons. They held their ground until their ammunition failed, when they were nearly all assegaied.

As I said before, what a private soldier knows about the plan of campaign is what he picks up from hearsay.

It soon leaked out that our fort was itself surrounded by Zulus, in such numbers that there was no possibility of leaving the place, either to go backward or forward, until reinforcements arrived. We were therefore put on short rations, and the small allowance of meat and flour which was doled out to us we cooked in various ways. For drinking purposes we had a small quantity of either tea, coffee, or lime juice; but we were altogether short of vegetables and tobacco.

I kept a diary while in Ekowe, and took note of the prices realised when the luxuries left behind by the mounted volunteers were put under the hammer, on the 22nd February 1879. Most of the goods were purchased by the officers, as prices were high: --

1½ lbs. tobacco	£1	9	0	1 small bottle of sauce	£1	1	0
1 small bottle of curry	0	14	0	1 pint of ketchup	0	15	6
1 large do.	1	7	0	1 box of sardines	0	11	0
7 cigars	0	9	0	1 bottle of ink	0	7	0
1 tin of condensed milk	0	14	6	1 pot salmon	0	15	6
1 do.	0	15	6	1 pot herrings	0	13	6
1 do.	0	18	0	1 lb. dubbin	0	9	6
1 do.	1	0	0	1 small packet of cocoa	0	11	0
1 tin of lobster .	0	13	6	1 ham (12 lbs.)	6	5	0
1 small bottle of pickles	1	6	0				

The last item, I remember, was knocked down to an officer of the 99th Regiment, who invited the Colonel to dine with him in the evening; but at the appointed time the feast was given up, for some person or persons unknown had stolen the joint!

We were now compelled to keep within the fort, except that occasionally we made raids in search of vegetables. Several times we visited native kraals, from which a few natives would fly on our approach, and here we sometimes found growing maize or pumpkins, which on our return we cooked and ate with much relish. But these raids were not unattended with danger, for frequently the Zulus would fire at us from the bush, and then there would be one or more wounded men to bring back, and place in the hospital tent. Each day, also, some of us were told off to guard the cattle outside the fort, and bring them back in safety at nightfall.

Doleful days were these; the rain used to come down in torrents, and we made our beds beneath the waggons, upon the damp ground, while creeping things crawled and ran over us as we slept. The officers used to sleep inside the waggons, and were, so far, a little more comfortable than the rank and file, but even they were roughing it.

We made the best of our time, now and then having an open-air concert, with choruses by all hands, at which times a few natives might be seen in the distance listening to our melodies; and now and then our marksmen would have a shot at them, for our rifles could reach them while theirs could not carry to us.

Sometimes the tables were turned, and frequently our mounted outposts would be attacked by Zulus, who crept up to them under cover of the long grass. One poor fellow rode back to the fort with more than a dozen wounds. How he managed to keep his seat and fight his way through the enemy I cannot tell. Those who fell into the hands of the Zulus were terribly mutilated, and left on the open ground to be found by their comrades on the following day, and carried back to the fort for burial.

That word "burial" reminds me of the funerals which so frequently took place, for typhoid fever came among us, and, despite the efforts of the doctors, carried off a good number of the men. The Rev. Mr. Ritchie, our chaplain, was a splendid man, and always hopeful and light-hearted. He attended all the funerals, none of which were very ceremonious; we simply wrapped the dead men in their blankets, and laid them in their graves without a parting volley, as ammunition was precious and we had no blank cartridges.

Time dragged wearily on, and there seemed no prospect of relief. Lieutenant Rowden, of the 99th Regiment, made several exploring expeditions, and ascertained the whereabouts of the Zulus; and on two or three occasions we captured from neighbouring kraals a considerable quantity of cattle, which were a welcome addition to our commissariat department.

Several of the Engineers who were with us manufactured a home-made heliograph, and were continually flashing signals to inform Lord Chelmsford of the desperate position we were in. For a long time these signals appeared to be unnoticed, but at last we learned that some reinforcements had arrived from St. Helena in *H.M.S. Shah*; and these, with a number of sailors forming part of the ship's crew, and others from *H.M.S. Boadicea*, together with 3300 whites, 1600 natives, and a small body of cavalry numbering about 160, with rocket tubes and ninepounders, were marching to our relief under Lord Chelmsford.

To this encouraging information our men replied, cautioning the advancing army that a force of Zulus, estimated at about 35,000, were prepared to bar their progress.

I think it was about the 2nd of April when the relieving column arrived at Ginghilovo, three-quarters of the distance to Ekowe, and here they formed a laager, threw up earthworks, dug shelter pits, and prepared to spend the night. At daybreak the sentries observed the enemy stealing round the camp, apparently making observations; and within an hour or two they were seen advancing, in their usual skirmishing order, with the horns extended on either side, ready to sweep round the camp and attack it upon all points.

The 60th Rifles were prepared for them at the front, and opened a terrific fire, so that the Zulus, notwithstanding their courage and recklessness, did not get within three hundred yards of the camp. Then they changed their front, and attacked the side of the camp held by the 57th and 91st Regiments, making four fierce charges, none of which brought them up to the line of bayonets.

They then made a last attack on the left of the camp, where they came within ten or fifteen feet of the muzzles of the men's rifles, a few bold spirits even rushing forward and catching hold of the latter, and stabbing at the soldiers with their assegais. But the British lines stood firm, and as the enemy retired the handful of cavalry charged out upon them, worrying them as they fled.

We heard later on that the loss of the Zulus was close upon a thousand, while the British lost three killed, and had thirty-seven wounded.

Though we could hear the fighting, we made no sortie, but simply waited until the relief came, and I shall never forget that relief as long as I retain my wits. It *was* good to grasp the hands of men who had risked their lives for us, and how we did enjoy a "square meal" and a smoke. Our friends had brought provi-

sions, but had carefully avoided overloading themselves. Early the next morning we made a successful raid on the kraal of a chief named Dabulamanzi, situated a few miles from Ekowe, and having procured some provisions, with payment in lead, we set out on our return journey to the Tugela.

As we turned our backs upon Ekowe, in which we had spent between seventy and eighty days, the Engineers blew up the fort, so as to leave nothing of which the Zulus could take advantage. We made it a rule to destroy all kraals which we passed on our march, so that our track was marked with smouldering ruins.

These kraals are built something like old-fashioned straw bee-hives. Long thin sticks are stuck into the ground in a circle, and joined together at the top; grass, straw, and twigs are threaded through the sticks, like basket-work, until the whole is weather-tight, almost airtight, I expect, except for the small hole through which one has to crawl. The word kraal stands for either a village or a hut, for the huts are seldom built singly.

We had no adventures on the return march; and camping once more at the Tugela, we waited while Lord Chelmsford continued his march to Durban for the purpose of arranging a general invasion of Zululand on a larger scale, with better organisation. For we had found the people more difficult to deal with than we at first expected.

Resting by the river-side we found time to talk over what had happened, and we then learned further particulars of the massacre at Isandlwhana.

Some of us were fortunate enough to receive papers from home, and I suppose every paper was read and passed on for the benefit of others. No one but a soldier on foreign service has any idea of the full value of a newspaper.

At last Lord Chelmsford fixed the 2nd of June as the day

for the second general advance, which was to be made in three columns much strengthened. The first, being that with which I served, was, as on the last occasion, to proceed along the coast-road, with Durban, Fort Pearson, and Ginghilovo as its bases of operation. The second, or central column, was under Lord Chelmsford; and the third, or flying column, was commanded by General Wood.

While on the march, we learned that Sir Garnet Wolseley was to be sent out to take command over Lord Chelmsford, and was on his way on board *H.M.S. Forester.* I happened to be stationed at Port Durnford, assisting in landing stores, when the vessel arrived off the shore, but on account of the heavy sea running she returned to Durban, and disembarked Sir Garnet at that port.

Before he arrived at our camp, we were paraded and ordered to fire a general salute in honour of a victory gained by the second and third columns, and the destruction of the Zulu capital on the 4th of July.

On that day, the two British columns having met, -- whilst No. 1 had not overcome all its difficulties, -- took up a position near Ulundi, forming a large hollow square, with Gatling guns in the centre. Colonel Redvers Buller, who, with his cavalry, had done splendid service in reconnoitring the country, advanced and set the smaller kraals on fire. This opened the ball, and the Zulus at once commenced their attack in such numbers that the cavalry were after a while compelled to retire within the square. All assaults of the enemy were repulsed by steady volleys, and finally, seeing them wavering, Colonel Drury Lowe led a charge by the King's Dragoon Guards and scattered them in all directions.

Nothing then remained to be done but to destroy Cetewayo's kraals, and while this work was in progress, Mr. Archibald Forbes, the special correspondent of the Daily News, set off on an adventurous ride of thirty miles through the enemy's country, to report that the war was practically over.

The enemy's loss was estimated at fifteen thousand, while the English lost under a dozen, which, however, included Captain Wyatt-Edgell, and eighty wounded. The King fled from his capital, attended only by a few faithful followers, and after a wearisome chase he was run to earth on the 29th of August, and escorted to Cape Town, where, with a few wives to share his captivity, he was allowed to reside as a political prisoner.

The Buffs were sent for two years to the Straits Settlements, and three years in Hong Kong; after which we returned to England, and I quitted the army.

Tommy Atkins' War Stories: 12

From Sebastopol to Lucknow

By Sergeant John Palmer

20th Regiment

Sergeant John Palmer saw action
with the Lancashire Fusiliers
in the Crimea and during
the Indian Mutiny.

From Sebastopol
to Lucknow

I enlisted at Chatham in the year 1849, joining the 20th
Regiment of Foot, which is now called the 2nd Lancashire Fusiliers. The regiment was afterwards stationed at Winchester, and
at the latter end of July 1854 at Plymouth, when we embarked
for the Crimea, being then one thousand eight hundred and
seventy-four bayonets, besides forty sergeants, drummers, band,
and staff.

I forget the name of the vessel that took us out, but she was a
large steamer, and was afterwards burnt at Liverpool, having just
landed a number of invalids.

The first battalion of the Rifle Brigade was in another vessel,
and we kept pretty well together during the voyage; but cholera
broke out among us when near Constantinople, and, having
obtained permission from the Sultan, we landed and encamped
at a place called Joshua's Valley, where we lost several men.

On re-embarking we sailed for Eupatoria, where the vessels
assembled and made a splendid show, dropping anchor all about
the same time. The busy little cadet boats, or pinnaces, were flying up and down between the lines, and to and from the vessels
with orders and despatches; and at a certain time, apparently
without giving signals from one ship to another, the whole of
the troops commenced to land.

Never shall I forget that night, which was one of the worst
I ever spent. The wind and rain made us most miserable, the
sea ran high, and many of the men-of-war's boats were driven
ashore and broken up by the surf. With the splinters from these

we managed somehow to get a fire alight, and then piling up the wreckage from the boats, we soon had a good blaze, and started fires all along the beach, around which we crowded, warming our limbs and drying our clothes.

As I was in General Gathcart's division I didn't have much to do at the first battle (the Alma). We were employed on the left flank at the foot of the hills, keeping off the Cossacks, who otherwise would have worked round and attacked our men in the rear.

After the battle, one of our officers, who spoke Russian, talked to an officer of the Imperial Guard who was taken prisoner, and he said that they had intended to keep us at bay for three weeks, and then drive us into the sea. He added, "We expected to find red British soldiers, but there were no soldiers among you; you were all red devils. However, you won't take Sebastopol, for that is impregnable." To this bit of brag our officer replied, "You haven't held your position three hours, let alone three weeks; and we shall see what luck you will have at Sebastopol."

After partaking of some refreshments, I was sent out with a party distributing rum and water to the wounded, no matter whether they were friends or foes; and at the end of three days all our dead were buried, and the wounded taken down to the ships, and transported to the hospital at Scutari.

On the 23rd we set out for Sebastopol, passing on the way through numbers of vineyards, and, as the grapes were not quite ripe, the order was "fifty lashes for the man caught eating them." This was done to prevent illness, and it doesn't take long to hold a drumhead court-martial on the field. There was also an order against looting, but we found the French helping themselves to potatoes, and somehow we forgot the order, and the officers forgot it too and were glad to share them with us.

Our attack on Balaklava was a strange affair. At our first shot a few soldiers in the town hoisted a flag of truce, and we took them all prisoners.

On arriving at the tableland above Sebastopol, the fourth division, under General Cathcart, flanked round to the right from Balaklava, and took up a position on the heights overlooking the town; while the second, third, and light divisions bivouacked in the valley of Balaklava.

It was nearly dark when we piled arms, and, without taking off any accoutrements, a few of us looked about to find some wood, and managed to get a fire to boil some rice for supper.

While we were standing round, enjoying the warmth, the General came up and asked us for a light. One of the men answered, "Can't you help yourself?" whereupon the General lighted his cigar at the fire, and we saw then who our visitor was, and immediately stood at attention! He said, "I think you've got a hard cheek to give them a light to fire at; but go on with your cooking; if you're not afraid, I'm not. If I have my will, those of us who are left will sup inside the town tomorrow night."

Almost before he had finished speaking a shower of bullets struck the ground in front of us and rebounded over our heads, whereupon the order was to put out fires and move about three hundred yards to the right; and after that no one was allowed to strike a light, and we had a cold supper.

The following morning Sir George formed our division in battle array in front of the town, and sent an orderly to Lord Raglan, saying, "If you will show a front on top of the hill, I can take the town with my division." The order came, "Fall back, pile arms, put outlying pickets, and wait for orders."

Lieutenant Chapham of the 20th said that if it hadn't been for that order we should have been home by Christmas. He was the man that built the half-moon battery which did so much execution in the town. He would never leave it, was in it night and day, and at last was killed in it.

A day or two after, I was sent with a large body of our men down the Woronzoff Road, to drive back some Cossacks who we heard were coming up. We remained out all day, and were about two hundred yards from the men who were raising the Malakhoff. Thousands of them were working with picks, shovels, and barrows, and as they had no arms or ammunition to protect themselves, and we had outflanked them, we could, if we had been allowed to fire a volley and then charge them, have driven them into our lines and taken them all prisoners. Our pickets always went within two hundred or three hundred yards of the Malakhoff and Redan, and yet we were never allowed to fire a shot. It almost makes me mad to think of it even now.

The three other divisions took up positions on our right, leaving the 93rd Highlanders at Balaklava to protect the cavalry, who were useless at the front except as orderlies.

I believe Lord Raglan's reason for delay was that, in his opinion, we should be able to reduce the town to submission by starvation and bombardment, and thus save the slaughter which would occur in storming the town; but this idea turned out to be a fallacy, for we allowed them to throw up earthworks which were almost impregnable.

The siege-guns were disembarked in Balaklava Harbour, but unfortunately we had no horses to drag them up the steep slopes, on to the plateau between the two towns. The bluejackets made light of this difficulty, and I have seen eighty or a hundred harnessed to a Lancaster gun, a sixty-eight pounder, dragging and tugging away in the best of spirits, while one of their number sat on the muzzle of a gun scraping a fiddle or blowing a flute. They were the merriest fellows out.

It was, I believe, about the 27th or 28th of September that we began to throw up our breastworks and build Green Hill battery, under the direction of the sappers, while others were employed in making fascines to assist in the work. Everything was ready to commence action by the 14th of October; and the French were ready before us, having better ground to work on.

At a given signal the whole of the ships of the fleet, and all the guns in the trenches, opened fire upon Sebastopol; the English guns being principally directed on the Round Tower, which had caused us considerable annoyance during our work, and it was silenced in ten minutes.

The sailors worked the siege-guns, and without much delay managed to blow up a Russian magazine; while all the men not engaged in the trenches ran to the front of the heights and gave them a hearty cheer. About an hour later there was another explosion, and we ran forward and cheered again, but were surprised to learn that this time it was one of our own magazines, close by the windmill, that had exploded. Nevertheless the cheer had a good effect, for the Russians ceased firing for two or three hours, and we could never otherwise account for it.

One morning, immediately after being relieved from the trenches, having just got our fires alight and rice boiling, the "Alarm" and "Assembly" sounded. You can imagine with what pleasure we took up our arms, fell in, and marched towards Balaklava in order to repel an expected attack; but the Cossacks, seeing us rushing down the hill, beat a retreat, and we saw no more of them that day.

We used to have twenty-four hours in the trenches at a time, always on the alert, and always in danger of being hit. There were many strange sights to be seen in those days. I remember once seeing a round shot from the Russians rolling along apparently so harmlessly that a man tried to stop it with his hands, but there was such a twist on the ball that, incredible as it may seem, his arms and legs were broken, and he was dead in a few minutes. Another man I saw put out his foot to stop a round shot that seemed to be almost spent, and it snapped his leg off just below his knee.

The misery of those days in the trenches will never be forgotten by those who had to endure them. I have seen men hold their hands above the parapet, hoping to have a shot through them so as to be invalided home rather than endure such wretchedness. I had to check several for so doing; and then they would pretend to be asleep, with an arm stretched out above their heads, so that if a shot came it might appear accidental. I can't call to mind all the hardships we endured, but I remember once, while eating a biscuit and a piece of salt pork, a man lying next to me was struck in the head with a piece of shell, and his brains were splashed on to my biscuit. I thought so little of it at the time that I wiped the biscuit and finished my meal. It was that or none.

Returning from the trenches on the morning of the 25th, after the usual twenty-four hours' duty in them, I was busy cooking some rice, when the "Alarm" and "Assembly" sounded, and we formed up and double-marched towards Balaklava. It was a beautifully fine day, and while marching down the hill we saw the whole of the light cavalry charge.

On arriving in the valley we formed line and lay down, covering our battery of artillery, which commenced firing at a two-gun redoubt on the left attack. This redoubt had been held by the Turks, but they had been driven out by an overwhelming number of Russians, who were then endeavouring to find our magazine. This they succeeded in doing after firing a few shots, and up it went. We had orders to charge and take the redoubt at the point of the bayonet, which we did under cover of the smoke from the explosion of our magazine.

When we got inside the redoubt we found nothing but a heap of dead and dying Turks. We had to remain here until the close of the engagement. The taking of that redoubt led to the recapture of the redoubt on the right attack by the first battalion of the Rifle Brigade.

One Saturday morning, as we were being relieved from the trenches, the Russians opened a tremendous fire, whereby five men of my company were wounded. We could not imagine how they had found out the hour at which we relieved our covering parties; however, about nine in the morning, a comrade and I went over to the canteen in the camp of the Royal Sappers and Miners, which was kept by two Maltese. As we could not find the shanty, we asked a sapper, and he pointed out the ruins of the place, and told us that the French had discovered these fellows giving information to the enemy, and had just been over and demolished their canteen and hung the traitors amid the ruins.

After this there was always heavy firing about relief time, sometimes rendering it impossible to leave the trenches, where we frequently had to remain for forty-eight hours at a stretch.

Early in the morning of the 5th of November the company to which I belonged came out from the trenches and took over the inlying picket. Everything went on as usual until we heard firing, and the word was passed, "Stand to your arms, inlying picket." We remained thus for some time, when, the firing getting heavier towards the town, the "Assembly" sounded from the headquarters of the division. This was a signal for all the regiments to turn out. The morning was terribly foggy, and Sir George Cathcart, passing by us, asked, "Is that you, Colonel Home?" Our Colonel answered, "Yes." Sir George replied, "Then take command; something is going to happen to me today, for I've forgotten my cigar." He galloped back, and some time before we had reached the windmill he had rejoined us, smoking his cigar as usual. I suppose it was his last, for he and Generals Strangeways, Goldie, and Torrens were among the slain that day.

Just after passing the mill, an officer, who I believe was His Royal Highness the Duke of Cambridge, came riding up, and asked, "What division is this?" On discovering Sir George Cathcart, he asked if he would give the order "Front turn, charge, and support the Guards." We came to a dead halt, but could see nothing of the fight, except a few of the Rifles lying near us firing.

I believe it was the Duke who gave the order "Run over the Rifles," and directly we did so we found ourselves face to face with a large body of Russians. What a time of excitement that was! Away we went at them like a line of lions, and charged them past the two-gun redoubt. They were so numerous that we were repulsed, but we rallied and charged them again. This time into the redoubt we went, and drove them out of it; but we could not hold it, for a ship called the *Twelve Apostles*, which had been sunk across the harbour to prevent our ships entering, and whose deck was nevertheless above water, could clear the fort with her shells, and whenever we were in possession of that redoubt they made it too hot to hold us, but when the Russians regained possession the ship ceased firing. We could never understand how this was managed.

The struggle round this little redoubt was terrible; we charged the enemy again and again. Just as I was making a point at a Russian, my foot slipped, and instead of giving a wound I received one in my thigh. It was, however, only slight, for my comrade, poor old Jesse Patient, shot the man dead; and away we went again, charging over the redoubt and down the ravine some distance.

When we fell back Jesse got captured, and as he had always said he wouldn't be taken alive, I suppose he had a good fight for liberty, for after the fight some of our men found his body dreadfully cut about, and they buried him with the others. Poor chap!

We charged down the ravine several times, but at last the

Russians came up in overpowering numbers, and we had to retire from the two-gun battery; but to our joy we found the French advancing to our support, and, with an English cheer, we charged the enemy once again and drove them back. They never recovered that charge, but retired into the town.

I was following them up, shouting and yelling like a fiend, when I received a bullet through the thick part of my leg and another in my arm, and over I went. I was picked up soon afterwards and taken to Balaklava Harbour, and from there to Scutari Hospital, whence, after a long stay, I was sent home to England, and rejoined my regiment.

The latter part of my yarn deals with India. We were stationed at Aldershot when news of the Mutiny arrived, and we were ordered to hold ourselves in readiness to proceed to the East. On the 3rd of August 1857 we marched to Farnborough, and went by rail to Portsmouth, where we embarked on the *Champion of the Seas* sailing vessel, and after a tedious voyage entered the river and were towed up to Garden Reach, Calcutta.

After a little delay we took train and proceeded to the end of the line, about eighty miles distant, and from thence we marched to Benares by detachments. When the whole of the regiment had arrived, we marched on to Jubbulpore, and relieved a detachment of the 10th Regiment. Here we received orders to advance towards Lucknow, and on our way we came across several camping-grounds of the mutineers.

While passing a large sugar plantation, where they had taken up a position, we had a good brush with them. However, a troop of mounted Sikhs who were with us surrounded the plantation, and set it on fire all round, so that all who were hidden inside it were destroyed.

We pushed on towards Sultanpore through a dense jungle, from which we emerged upon a large plain with a strong fort in the centre of it, which immediately opened fire on us. We formed into line, with our best marksmen in front, and under a burning sun we boldly advanced and drove the mutineers from the fort at the point of the bayonet, capturing no less than twenty-one big guns.

As soon as the fight was over we threw ourselves down to rest, but suddenly an artillery officer galloped up to where I was and asked us to come and help his men as they had a nine-pounder disabled. We crossed the plain at a steady double for about two miles, for we all knew the value of the gun, having only three of them with us. We soon got the gun ready for action again, and marched back to the column; but the terrible heat made us all call out for the *beasties* (bihistis), or native water-carriers, and we were glad to pile arms and rest for the night.

The next morning, being off duty, I wandered round the battlefield, where I found that we had done more execution than I at first expected. The dead lay in heaps, just as if our shrapnel shells had burst in the midst of columns of them. Our artillery were busy collecting and bursting all the captured guns.

After this we had a wearying march across country till we arrived outside Lucknow, and for three days we faced the college, which was well loopholed and in possession of the rebels. In the afternoon of the third day, up came our bluejackets with their guns, and commenced a fire upon the college which soon silenced it; but they lost their brave leader, Captain Peel, R.N.

Next day we advanced farther into the town, and came upon the Royal Artillery, stationed in an enclosed plain, with a number of mortars, with which they were shelling the town. From here we pushed on and captured a cavalry barracks, where we remained for the night, and at daylight advanced still farther. The excitement was intense, and it seemed as if the whole of our troops were on the move.

I was told that Sir Colin Campbell intended to advance as far as the officers' mess of the 32nd Regiment, but we were halted close to the old palace, on the banks of the river. The next morning we passed through the palace, and took possession of the stone and iron bridges; and on the following day the whole town was in our possession, except the farther portions of the outskirts.

Next day we took up our position in the Grand Bazaar, but every shop was closed. We remained here two or three days; and then, I remember, Sir James Outram came and asked our Colonel to send a few of us up and down the different streets to tell the people that they might open their shops and that our troops would protect them.

We went up and down several side streets, and then got back into the bazaar again about three hundred yards from where we started. Sir James, who was with us, halted and looked round to see in which direction to proceed, when all of a sudden about a dozen musket shots came flying amongst us, and we discovered about a score of rebels a hundred yards or so away, one of them being dressed in a Highlander's uniform.

Sir George ordered me to run back for a few more men, and I started off as fast as I could, crossing from one side of the street to the other, for the blacks kept up a sharp fire after me. I got to the main body all right, and soon brought back a reinforcement.

We were met with a volley, and had orders to get under cover near a large building which crossed the street with an archway. One of the mutineers was a splendid shot, for he popped out of his corner, fired, and popped back again, and every shot told. Seven of our men were hit, and our Captain also received a graze on his cheek, whereupon he gave orders for us to charge through the archway, which we did. We came out upon a large open street, in the centre of which was one of our nine-pounder brass guns, with a fellow standing at the breech, blowing a slow-match, ready to fire on us. Our Sergeant (Corbett) dropped on his knee, took cool aim and fired, and the man leaped into the air and fell dead. Charging down, we captured the gun, turned it round, and poured the contents into the retreating rebels.

The men then dragged the gun to headquarters with me seated on the muzzle. After this we were quartered in the old palace for three weeks or longer: and here a Hindoo, who spoke good English, and was always cursing the Sepoy rebels, used to come round selling fruit. One night we were marched out into the country for a long distance, and at daybreak we came upon a large body of mutineers cooking their breakfast. Our horse artillery opened fire and drove them off, and the first scoundrel I saw lying dead was the fruit seller, who had given them notice of all our movements. After that we were a little more careful of strange faces.

For the next few months we had nothing but marching, skirmishing, and one or two good fights; always keeping a sharp lookout for the enemy, and always glad to be in pursuit of them. They were but poorly armed, some had only a sword, some had matchlocks, and very few had muskets, so that we had light work to drive them before us and cut them down.

At last the country became quiet, and I was not sorry to get back to old England to end my days in peace.

Sent to Save Gordon

By Harry Etherington

Royal Sussex

Harry Etherington describes service with the Camel Corps and at the battle of Abu Klea during the attempted relief of Gordon and Khartoum.

Sent to Save Gordon

I had been two years in garrison at Malta, when, on a fearfully hot day in July 1884, there came the news that some of us were wanted for the expedition which was on its way to rescue General Gordon, who was at that time a prisoner in Khartoum.

Volunteers were asked for, and you may be sure that nearly every man wanted to go. Not only was it an agreeable prospect to get away from Malta and have a change of scene, but there was the chance of gaining honours and promotion in active service. Above all, every man was anxious that the hero in Khartoum should be saved from the terrible danger which threatened him.

We crossed over to Cairo, and from there we set out in the native boats, or *dahabeahs*, for Assouan, at the first cataract, where we were to join our first battalion.

The very evening we went on board one of our men was drowned while swimming; and a few hours later, when we were all asleep on deck, one of the soldiers, who had been drinking hard, suddenly started up in a dream and threw himself overboard. The confusion which followed was indescribable. No sooner was the splash heard and an alarm given than our men sprang up, thinking that the enemy was boarding us under cover of the darkness. We were moored to the bank, and the native soldiers bolted as soon as the alarm was given.

For the next few minutes a very dangerous state of things prevailed. To put it plainly, we were uncommonly frightened. Every man seized his bayonet, and as in the darkness we could not tell friend from foe, and the men at each end of the boat thought that the enemy was at the other, it is a great wonder that we did not kill one another by mistake. But happily Captain Harding appeared on the scene with a revolver, and soon restored order. The man who had jumped overboard was rescued by one of his comrades.

At Assouan we joined our regiment, which now numbered about seven hundred men, and here the expedition was formed and set out for Sarras, near Wady Haifa. From Sarras we went up the Nile in dahabeahs to Dongola, and now it was that the hardships really began.

We were the pioneer expedition, and consequently we had to rough it, I can assure you. Each of our companies was on a separate dahabeah, and owing to the numerous bends in the river the wind would help some and hinder others, so that we got very much scattered. The living was simply shocking. Our biscuits were swarming with maggots, and the tinned "bully beef" had not been improved by the hot weather. Still, however badly it smelt, we were glad to eat it, for we had nothing else but Egyptian lentils and horse beans. We had to drink the water of the Nile, which was about the colour of coffee; and many of our men suffered severely from diarrhoea and dysentery, and several died. Only one surgeon was with us, and, owing to the dahabeahs becoming scattered, he could not attend to us all.

The current of the Nile was six knots an hour, and we had to do a lot of rowing, which was fearfully exhausting work, to say nothing of blistered hands. Then our clothes and boots wore out; and altogether we were glad when we reached Dongola on 22nd October, after being a month on the voyage.

Here we were met by the Mudir, with a crowd of friendly natives, who rushed down to the river bank carrying the heads of Mahdist rebels on their spears. I was the first to land, and I believe I am right in saying that I was the first Englishman who ever entered Dongola.

We found quite a large town, surrounded by a trench and wall, and here we waited a month for reinforcements. Before this time had expired, Lord Wolseley, who had been appointed to the command, arrived on the scene, having hurried up the Nile in a steamer. I was on guard outside his quarters when he arrived, and the first thing he said was this -- "My man, if you feel very hot you need not walk up and down; keep in the shade of a date-palm." I shall never forget his kind and considerate ways.

At the end of the month reinforcements arrived. They came up the Nile in whaling boats, which had been brought from England for the purpose. Poor fellows! They were in a pretty state. Their hands were raw with rowing, and their trousers had been worn to rags against the seats of the boats. Some of the men had actually patched their trousers with pieces of tin from the biscuit boxes!

The expedition now numbered five thousand men, and we all set out in whalers for Korti, except a small garrison left behind at Dongola. We were a week on the way, and had a hard time of it. Rowing is weary work at the best of times, and when the river is full of rocks which threaten to upset you, and swarming with crocodiles which long to devour you, it is really no joke. We were not sorry when we reached the little village of Korti.

Here we spent Christmas Day, and I wished myself back in England. In the morning we had service, but I was not present, because I was on fatigue duty carrying ammunition all day long. Each man had a ration of flour served out to make him a date-pudding, but as we had no suet our cookery was nothing to boast of. We also had a ration of rum, -- the last intoxicant that any of us got during the campaign, -- but it was only a thimbleful, so that nobody was any the worse for it. In the evening we had a sing-song, with Lord Wolseley in the chair.

But a sad gloom was cast over our Christmas Day by the arrival of a message from General Gordon -- the last that he was able to send. It was only a postage-stamp, secretly brought by a native runner, and on the back of it were simply the words, "Gordon can hold out no longer." Every man of us was eager to press on then.

We only stayed at Korti long enough to build a fort and to organise a camel corps. Oh, those camels! I shall never forget them. They were the mangiest set of brutes that ever walked. Nearly all of them were diseased and swarming with maggots, while the stench was simply unbearable. Learning to ride them was no treat either. I was no sooner on than I was off, and that was the case with most of us. But we soon managed to control the brutes, and then we set out as a flying column to cross the desert at full speed for Khartoum.

We were fifteen hundred strong, and consisted of eight companies of the Royal Sussex, the 19th Hussars, the heavy Camel Corps, a hundred Marines, the Naval Brigade, and the Royal Artillery.

While we were crossing the desert, Major-General Earle went round the river with the 46th and 75th Regiments, hoping to reach Metemmeh, where it was believed that General Gordon had some steamers, by which means Khartoum might be reached by water.

We started from Korti on 8th January 1885, and had a terrible journey across the desert. Each man was allowed only two pints of water a day for all purposes, and carried it in a pigskin, which usually burst and let the contents escape. We each carried sufficient rations of "bully beef" and biscuit to last a hundred days.

The heat was appalling, and the sandstorms in the desert

were terrible. When they came on we could do nothing but dismount and crouch behind the kneeling camels, while the driving sand filled our eyes and ears and noses.

We passed but few wells on the way, and these were mainly stagnant. On the 13th we reached Gakdul Wells, where one man in his eagerness for water fell in and was killed. Here it was that I first saw Colonel Burnaby. He was a magnificent man in native dress, and how he got here in the midst of the desert I don't know. Here, too, we began to find traces of the enemy -- footprints in the sand, and ashes of camp-fires still warm. But we saw nothing of the natives themselves.

Two days before reaching Abu Klea my camel broke down from sheer exhaustion, and I had to tramp all day long through the burning sand. At last I got another camel, and a drink of water. But my troubles were not yet over. When the rear column came up they found my camel dead, and my blanket and rations stolen. Then the new camel bolted, and carried me two miles on the reverse flank of the column, finally throwing me and my goods into a sandhole, where I remained till I was fetched by an escort. By this adventure I lost all my kit as well.

On January 16th we approached Abu Klea Wells, which are situated in a defile between some low hills. We brought up for dinner three miles off in the desert, and sent forward a party of Hussars to see if the wells were occupied. As they did not return, General Stewart ordered an advance, when all at once there were shouts of "Dismount! Undo ammunition!" and we saw the Hussars riding back for their lives, and announcing that the Mahdists were thousands strong at the wells.

We were at once formed into a three-sided square, with the camels in the middle; one man being told off to look after six camels. Then we began to advance over the broken ground. About two miles from the wells it became dusk, and just as the sun was setting on the skyline we saw the gleam of hundreds of native spears on the brow of a low hill. Some sharp shooting followed, but we were too far off to do any good, and in a few minutes it was dark.

Then commenced a night of terror. We formed a zereba of bushes and crouched behind it; many a man prayed that night who was not in the habit of doing so, I can assure you. You see it is one thing to face a foe in the field, and quite another to lie awake all night expecting to be killed every minute. All the while the Mahdists kept up a desultory firing -- for they had two thousand Remingtons, captured from Hicks Pacha -- and we lost several men and a number of camels.

All night long we could hear the native tom-toms beating, and every moment we expected a charge. I was told off for outpost duty, which was not very pleasant under the circumstances, but we did not go more than a hundred yards from the column. My regiment was in the rear, the heavy Camel Corps being in front. Colonel Burnaby came round to us all, and said, "Don't strike a light, and don't fire on any account, or you will show the enemy where you are; wait till you see the white of their eyes, and then bayonet them."

By this time we were almost maddened with thirst, for our supply of water was nearly exhausted and we had only a pint per man left. Hence it was absolutely necessary that we should capture the wells before we went any farther.

The next morning we had one of those glorious sunrises that are only to be seen in the tropics. At eight o'clock we again formed square, for the Mahdists were beginning to descend from the hills. We sent out skirmishers to attack them, and Lieutenant de Lisle was shot while we were forming square.

The enemy then formed in three columns of five thousand men each, with riflemen on each side, the rest being armed with spears, and all thoroughly well disciplined.

We were only two deep in square till within fifty yards of

the enemy, when our skirmishers retired, and we opened square to let them in. At that moment the Mahdists charged, but were repulsed. A second charge failed, but at the third they succeeded in breaking one corner of the square, and then the position became very serious indeed. Probably their success was due to the fact that our men at that corner were not used to the bayonet but to the sword. Anyhow, the Soudanese broke a British square, and that is something to their credit.

Our seven-pounders were thus left outside, and Colonel Burnaby rushed out of the square to recapture them. He fought like a hero, but was thrust in the throat by a Mahdist spearman and killed. We dragged him back into the square, but it was too late.

It was at this point that Gunner Smith won the only Victoria Cross of the campaign. When the square was broken, Major, Guthrie stuck to the guns, and fought till he fell wounded. Then Gunner Smith rushed to the rescue. He had lost his rifle, but he caught up a gun spike, beat off the Soudanese, and dragged the Major back into the square.

When the square was re-formed a lot of the Mahdists were inside, but you may be sure that none of them lived to get out again. One odd incident happened inside the square. We were carrying a number of chests of bullion for Gordon, and these were knocked open in mistake for ammunition, so that the ground was literally strewn with sovereigns.

At last the Gatling guns were got into action, and that practically ended the battle. The Soudanese were simply mown down. Their bodies flew up into the air like grass from a lawn-mower. But their pluck was astonishing. I saw some of the natives dash up to the Gatling guns, and thrust their arms down the muzzles, trying to extract the bullets which were destroying their comrades! Of course, they were simply blown to atoms. The battle lasted off and on from eight in the morning till five in the afternoon, when the Soudanese finally fled. We did not pursue them, but with a ringing cheer we dashed to the wells, for we had drunk nothing all day, and were nearly maddened with thirst. Altogether sixty-five of our men were killed, and a hundred and eighty wounded, while about two thousand natives lay dead upon the sand.

We buried Colonel Burnaby where he fell, and every uninjured man brought the biggest stone he could find, and so we built a great cairn over the man who died as a volunteer in the service of his country.

The next day was Sunday, and after service, which was conducted by General Stewart, we built a fort of stones. Here my company stayed with the wounded, while the rest of the column pushed on to Metemmeh.

We were here two months in the desert. We had no tents, but simply lay out on the sands, never undressing for weeks. For food we were dependent upon what was sent from Metemmeh, and sometimes that was not overmuch. On one occasion we were glad to kill a donkey and eat it, while the hyenas and jackals prowled around the camp.

During this time Khartoum fell, and General Gordon was killed. The news was kept from the troops for some time, but when at last it was made known there was not a dry eye in the camp. Strong men cried like children when they heard that their hero was dead.

After the fall of Khartoum, sixty thousand Mahdists advanced on Metemmeh, causing the British force -- now numbering about two thousand men, with General Buller in command -- to fall back on Abu Klea. The enemy followed and encamped about half a mile from us. Here they hung about and perpetually harassed us. We sent out skirmishers to try to draw them out of their encampment, but without success.

One day in March, news came that the Mahdists were going

to attack us at four o'clock in the morning, and General Buller arranged a plan to outwit them. The camp fires were lit as usual when night came on, and all the customary sounds were kept up, so that nothing unusual might be suspected. Then under cover of the darkness our men stole out of the camp, one company at a time, and went silently away to a place three miles off. In the morning a party of Hussars was sent to harass the Soudanese, in the hope of drawing them out into the open, where we were waiting for them, but they were too wide-awake to be drawn into the trap. So the British troops returned to the Gakdul Wells. Here General Stewart died of his wounds, and over his grave we erected a little wooden cross. Then we returned to Korti, having done the whole journey on foot, for all our camels were dead. Our boots were worn out and our clothes were in rags, and it was no joke to toil across one hundred and seventy-five miles of yielding sand, under a blazing African sun. But we got to Korti at last, and stayed there till the autumn, expecting to once more advance upon Khartoum.

But a change in the Home Government had altered the state of affairs, and we returned home instead, sad at heart that we had endured such hardships and lost so many comrades all for nothing, but sorrowing most of all that we had been sent too late to save General Gordon.

Tommy Atkins' War Stories: 14

On the March to Chitral

By George Pridmore

Bedfordshire Regiment

George Pridmore describes the expedition to relieve the beseiged garrison of Chitral on the North West Frontier of India

On the March
to Chitral

I went out to India with my regiment in 1891, and first heard about the Chitral Expedition on St. Patrick's Day, 17th March 1895.

It was Sunday morning, and we were on church parade at Peshawar when the news came, and we were told to be ready to march in twenty-four hours' time. Up till then we had heard nothing of the terrible danger which threatened the British agent, Surgeon-Major Robertson, and his gallant little band of native soldiers, in the besieged fort at Chitral. We had only heard a vague rumour that war was in the air.

The next twenty-four hours were pretty busy, I can assure you, for an enormous quantity of arrangements have to be made for a campaign in a wild country, cut off by high mountains from any centre of civilisation, but, of course, the burden of making these arrangements fell most heavily upon the officers.

We were ready in time, though no less than twenty-eight thousand pack animals -- mules and camels -- had to be collected to convey the baggage and food. You must remember that when war is carried on in a civilised country it is easy to buy or seize provisions on the road, but between Peshawar and Chitral the country consists of desolate mountains and wild valleys, with only small native villages at long intervals. It was necessary, therefore, to carry everything with us, yet matters were so well arranged that our baggage only amounted to ten pounds for each man and forty pounds for each officer.

For some reason our departure was delayed, and we remained under canvas till the 28th, when we started on a two days' march to Nowsbera, which was made the base of operations. On the following day we removed to Mardan, an eighteen miles' march. At least, it was officially called eighteen miles, but it really was a good deal more. Here the three brigades concentrated. The first, to which I belonged, consisted of the Bedfordshire Regiment, the 60th Rifles, the 15th Sikhs, and the 37th Dogras.

The march, which occupied six hours, was fearfully fatiguing. The sun was blazing hot, and the road was very dusty. Each of us carried his overcoat and a hundred rounds of ammunition, so that we were glad to buy lemonade from the natives whenever there was a chance. General Kinloch was in command of our brigade; General Sir Robert Low having command of the entire expedition. At Mardan we bivouacked for the night, each man lying out on the open ground.

The following morning we went on to Lundkwar, where we remained until the next day. The march was a very wearisome one, over hilly country where there was often no road. Sometimes we were following native tracks, at others crossing fields, and then again scrambling over rocks. As we carried no tents on this expedition (in order to reduce the baggage as much as possible), we had again to bivouac for the night.

This is unpleasant at the best of times in a tropical country. Not only are the nights very chilly, but the creeping things are simply legion. First there are the ants, which march over you in armies, and often get inside your clothes and bite desperately. Some species in particular seem to bite you with red-hot teeth. Then there are scorpions and centipedes, which sting and bite in a far worse fashion. I have known men suffer very severely for hours after being attacked by them. Of course, when you are lying out on the open ground at night, you are in constant danger from these creatures.

Wild beasts never come near the camp, except the jackals, which are not at all dangerous, though they are most shocking thieves. The man who has drawn his rations over night will probably find nothing but the smell left in the morning.

The night we spent at Lundkwar was more than usually trying, for it rained heavily, and we got quite wet through. Each of us had two blankets and a waterproof sheet. The latter is supposed to be used to keep us off the damp ground, but it is a common practice for two or three men to club together and construct a sort of gipsy tent with the aid of their sheets and some sticks. But when we lay down, the weather was fine, so that we took no precautions. In the morning you could see men everywhere sitting wrapped in blankets, with their clothes spread out to dry, and under these circumstances the British army did not present a very imposing spectacle.

In the morning we were hindered by the weather, and although the "Reveille" sounded at four o'clock it was nine before we set out for Shahkot, near the Malakhand Pass, which we were to storm.

There are three ways by which it is possible to cross the mountains which form the boundary of India at this point, and so to gain entrance to the Swat Valley, which lies on the road to Chitral. These are the Mora Pass, the Shahkot Pass, and the Malakhand Pass. Each of them is about three thousand five hundred feet high, and the path is about as rough as it well could be.

The General in command heard that all three passes were strongly held by hostile Swats, and he decided that the Malakhand Pass should be attacked. So he had ordered us to bivouac at Lundkwar, which is near the Shahkot Pass, in order to make the natives think that we were going to attack it, while a body of cavalry rode up to the Mora Pass to alarm the natives in that quarter. By this means he prevented the enemy from concentrating their forces on the Malakhand, which was the real point of attack.

It was on April 3rd that the battle, was fought, the very day -- as we afterwards heard -- when Colonel Kelly and his gallant little band of natives crossed the Shandhur Pass, far away to the north, struggling through five feet of snow, and actually carrying the cannon on their backs. Our 2nd Brigade led the attack under General Waterfield, the 1st Brigade acted as support, and the 3rd was held in reserve.

The Swats were about twelve thousand in number, about half of them being armed, and were spread over a mile and a half. They were stationed on the heights on either side of the pass, and had their *sangars* -- small breastworks of stone behind which to crouch and shoot -- ranged on all the spurs. Those who were not armed occupied themselves in rolling great stones down the steep mountain-side as our men rushed up to the attack. Our officers said that the position was such a strong one that a well-disciplined force might have held it for a week. As things were, it was captured after five hours' fighting.

First of all, the Guides and the 4th Sikhs were sent to climb the heights on the right, and then to attack the enemy's flank while the main charge was made in front. But so steep and rough was the climbing that they did not reach the top until the pass was practically won. In the meantime our three batteries were brought into action, and one by one the *sangars* on the hillsides were carefully shelled. Then the King's Own Scottish Borderers and the Gordon Highlanders advanced to the attack. They made a splendid dash up an almost perpendicular slope of more than a thousand feet, in the teeth of a perfect avalanche of stones, which the Swats were busily rolling down upon them.

Next the 1st Brigade set out, the 60th Rifles and the 15th Sikhs attacking in front, while the Bedfordshire and the 37th Dogras made for the enemy's left.

In this way the whole line got up near the pass. A short pause was made for the stragglers to get into position, and then bayonets were fixed and the "Charge" sounded. The three regiments then made a united dash for the crest, and with a great shout the position was carried at the point of the bayonet, and the pass was stormed.

The Swats fled in all directions, like chaff before the wind, and the Bedfordshire Regiment and the 37th Dogras pursued them down the farther valley till they reached the village of Khar, on the Swat River.

During the engagement about five hundred of the natives were killed, and nearly a thousand wounded; while we had less than seventy killed and wounded. The reason our loss was so small was just this. The Swat races are very poor marksmen. Their usual method is to sight their weapons for a certain mark beforehand, and they keep firing at this throughout the battle. If any of our men got within the line of fire they would probably be hit, but our method was first to send a few men forward to make a dust and induce the enemy to fire. Then we noticed where the bullets hit, kept just outside the mark, and picked off our opponents. In this way most of the enemy's fire proved a simple waste of powder and shot.

I was on convoy duty, much to my disappointment, so that I took no active part in storming the Malakhand Pass, but I had a fine view of the engagement. For five hours the Swats faced a most deadly fire without flinching, although we used mountain batteries, and they were largely armed with old flintlocks, and in some cases had to actually apply lighted matches to their rifles to make them go off. It is true that a certain number of them were armed with Martini-Henris and Sniders, but they could not use them to much effect.

How did they get these? Well, most of them were probably stolen from our troops in North India. These hill tribes are most expert thieves. They enter the camp at night without a sound, and, if any bungalow door has been left unlocked, something will be sure to have vanished before morning. I have known many a man to lose his rifle in this way. The thieves come naked and well oiled, so that if caught they nearly always wriggle out of our clutches and escape.

But they were wonderfully plucky in the fight. After the battle a good number of wounded natives came into camp for treatment, for I suppose you know that it is the custom in the British army to render full medical assistance to any wounded foes who care to avail themselves of it. Well, the number of wounds that some of these men carried was simply astonishing. One man had six bullets through him, and then walked nine miles to a village, where he was treated by one of our army surgeons, and actually recovered!

One man stood on the top of a hut and beat a tom-tom to encourage his comrades. Several times he dropped wounded, but each time struggled up again, until at last he was shot through the heart and fell headlong down the cliff. One of their standard-bearers was knocked over by our bullets again and again before he was finally killed.

One incident which occurred during the fight was especially remarkable. We noticed a man standing on a high peak with a signalling-flag. He had evidently belonged to some of our native troops, for he was an expert signaller, and as he watched our operations with the batteries -- which were now aimed at the sangars -- he signalled the result of each shot for the benefit of his comrades. Thus we saw him making the usual signals for "too high," "too low," "on the right," and so on, as the case might be. Of course that sort of thing was not convenient, so we sent a shell where we thought it would do most good, and blew the signaller all to pieces. The moment he was hit, another native sprang to the spot, caught up the flag, and signalled a bull's eye!

When the fight was over, the half-company, who had pursued the retreating Swats to Khar, camped for the night in the village. They had no food with them, but the natives, seeing who were the winning party, soon came with great professions of friendship and gave them rice and fruit, as well as straw for bedding and wood for fires. For a wonder the food was not poisoned, and our men spent a quiet night. In the meantime one company stayed in the pass for the night, and the rest of us bivouacked below it. Each man had a ration of biscuits, bully-beef, and rum.

About midnight we were called up and received orders to start at once and cross the pass in the dark. This was a most difficult business, as we had to get all our baggage along a narrow Buddhist road, which was nothing more than a rough footpath up the mountainside, and in many places was extremely steep. Halfway up we met a company of troops coming down for more baggage, and the result was that -- what with the crowding and the darkness -- we got hopelessly blocked for two hours, and did not reach the pass until eight o'clock in the morning. Here we had our breakfast of chupatties, rice, and tea, and then waited while the rest of the convoy struggled up the mountain.

It was a tremendous business to drag and push our heavy ammunition baggage over the pass. A lot of us were told off to improve the Buddhist road, which was said to be two thousand years old, and when we had cleared away the stones and filled up the holes, the work was not quite so difficult. But, it was still quite hard enough. We carried our bedding in great bundles strapped to the sides of the mules, our boots and coats being put inside the bedding. Every now and then we would come to a narrow place between two rocks, where the mule stuck fast. Under these circumstances he generally fell down and refused to move till we had unloaded him, and then he would roll and kick and struggle, while the whole company was brought to a

standstill. There is no creature on earth so wicked as a mule --
except a camel!

My company, which went across in the dark, lost forty-three
coats and bedding, besides a large number of boots. Many a
man found himself with only one boot next day. But most of
these things were found and brought along by the rear guard.

About one o'clock the whole column moved down to the
Swat Valley, which we reached at three o'clock.

While we were on the march, the 1st Brigade had gone on
ahead into the valley and was attacked by thousands of Swats,
who came rushing from the Shahkot and Mora Passes when
they found that the Malakhand had been taken. We could see
them in the plains in front, and on the spurs of the hills to the
right, waving flags, and evidently in a state of great excitement.
The 37th Dogras and the Mountain Artillery were sent forward
to hold them in check until we had got all our baggage clear of
the pass.

Towards evening, as we made no attack upon them, the enemy became bolder, and were evidently contemplating an open
attack upon us. Accordingly the few cavalry men who had now
crossed the pass were ordered to advance round the spur which
concealed us from the Swats, and to watch for an opportunity of
driving them back. This body of cavalry consisted of only fifty
sabers of the Guides under Captain Adams, who, with remarkable pluck and daring, at once charged the enemy and drove the
whole of them back into the mountains.

There were at this time about two thousand Swats in the
open, and the fact that fifty horsemen were able to drive them
back had a most terrifying effect upon them. The prompt success of this little party of Guides was no doubt largely due to
the fact that horse soldiers were quite unknown in the country,
and the natives had no idea that we could get them across the
pass. That so small a band was bold enough to charge forty times

their own number must have taken their breath away. At any rate the natives completely lost heart, and next morning they had disappeared from the neighbourhood. We only lost seven or eight of our men, but at least two hundred and fifty of the Swats were killed.

Some of the natives showed great spirit on this occasion, before the cavalry appeared on the scene. A few of them actually rushed upon the Dogras, and cut a man down before they could be driven off. While the fighting was going on we were entertained with the music of several stolen bugles, which the Swats evidently thought would assist them in gaining the victory!

When all had got quiet, we bivouacked in square for the night, with our baggage and mules inside.

As part of the bedding was still on the other side of the pass, we had a pretty uncomfortable time as we lay there in the open. Every man was fully dressed and armed, and we kept in square, as there was the probability that the Swats might try to attack us under cover of the darkness. But they had been too thoroughly scared, and the night passed quite quietly.

The next day all the rest of our baggage was brought over the pass, and then we made a reconnaissance towards Thana, where the enemy could be seen in large numbers. After this the 1st Brigade, to which I belonged, stayed at Khar to guard the Swat Valley, and great was our disappointment to find that we were not to share the perils and the glory of the 2nd and 3rd Brigades, which at once pushed forward towards Chitral.

On the 6th of April the main body prepared to cross the Swat River. About four thousand five hundred of the enemy were massed upon the low hills which come right down to the northern bank of the river, and were reinforced by a number of riflemen sent down by the rebel chief, Umra Khan, under command of his brother.

Now it was evident that to cross the river in the teeth of such a force would mean the loss of a large number of our men, so General Waterfield arranged a clever stratagem. While we harassed the enemy with our batteries from the south side of the river, the Guides Cavalry and the 11th Bengal Lancers went a long way up the river, crossed by a ford, and fell upon the flank and rear of the enemy.

This proved a most effective plan, for no sooner did the Swats see the dreaded horsemen dashing down upon them than they completely lost heart and were soon in full flight.

Preparations were at once made for crossing the river with the aid of inflated skins. This was a dangerous business, as the river was at that season a rushing torrent, and the men were up to their armpits. Two or three were washed away and drowned.

After this the main force moved on, and we saw no more of them. On the 13th a sharp fight took place on the banks of the Panjkora River, and on the 17th Umra Khan was defeated at Munda, and fled from the country, thus virtually ending the campaign.

It was on the following night that the besieged garrison at Chitral was relieved by the little band of Sikhs who formed Kelly's relief force, and who had accomplished one of the most remarkable marches on record. But no British soldiers fought at Chitral, and, with the exception of a very small advance guard, none of our men ever went so far.

We who were left behind at Khar stayed there till May 25th, and then went to a hill station at Laram Khotam for the hot season. There we remained till August 14th, when we returned to Rawal Pindi, and were once more on British territory.

Tommy Atkins' War Stories: Appendix
Tommy
By Rudyard Kipling

Tommy

I went into a public-'ouse to get a pint o' beer,
The publican 'e up an' sez, "We serve no red-coats here."
The girls be'ind the bar they laughed an' giggled fit to die,
I outs into the street again an' to myself sez I:
   O it's Tommy this, an' Tommy that, an' "Tommy, go away";
   But it's "Thank you, Mister Atkins", when the band begins to play,
   The band begins to play, my boys, the band begins to play,
   O it's "Thank you, Mister Atkins", when the band begins to play.

I went into a theatre as sober as could be,
They gave a drunk civilian room, but 'adn't none for me;
They sent me to the gallery or round the music-'alls,
But when it comes to fightin', Lord! they'll shove me in the stalls!
   For it's Tommy this, an' Tommy that, an' "Tommy, wait outside";
   But it's "Special train for Atkins" when the trooper's on the tide,
   The troopship's on the tide, my boys, the troopship's on the tide,
   O it's "Special train for Atkins" when the trooper's on the tide.

Yes, makin' mock o' uniforms that guard you while you sleep
Is cheaper than them uniforms, an' they're starvation cheap;
An' hustlin' drunken soldiers when they're goin' large a bit
Is five times better business than paradin' in full kit.
   Then it's Tommy this, an' Tommy that, an' "Tommy, 'ow's yer soul?"
   But it's "Thin red line of 'eroes" when the drums begin to roll,
   The drums begin to roll, my boys, the drums begin to roll,
   O it's "Thin red line of 'eroes" when the drums begin to roll.

We aren't no thin red 'eroes, nor we aren't no blackguards too,
But single men in barricks, most remarkable like you;
An' if sometimes our conduck isn't all your fancy paints,
Why, single men in barricks don't grow into plaster saints;
  While it's Tommy this, an' Tommy that, an' "Tommy, fall be'ind",
  But it's "Please to walk in front, sir", when there's trouble in the wind,
  There's trouble in the wind, my boys, there's trouble in the wind,
  O it's "Please to walk in front, sir", when there's trouble in the wind.

You talk o' better food for us, an' schools, an' fires, an' all:
We'll wait for extry rations if you treat us rational.
Don't mess about the cook-room slops, but prove it to our face
The Widow's Uniform is not the soldier-man's disgrace.
  For it's Tommy this, an' Tommy that, an' "Chuck him out, the brute!"
  But it's "Saviour of 'is country" when the guns begin to shoot;
  An' it's Tommy this, an' Tommy that, an' anything you please;
  An' Tommy ain't a bloomin' fool -- you bet that Tommy sees!

Rudyard Kipling

ALSO FROM LEONAUR
AVAILABLE IN SOFTCOVER OR HARDCOVER WITH DUST JACKET

RGW1 RECOLLECTIONS OF THE GREAT WAR 1914 - 18
STEEL CHARIOTS IN THE DESERT by S. C. Rolls

The first world war experiences of a Rolls Royce armoured car driver with the Duke of Westminster in Libya and in Arabia with T.E. Lawrence.

SOFTCOVER : **ISBN 1-84677-005-X**
HARDCOVER : **ISBN 1-84677-019-X**

RGW2 RECOLLECTIONS OF THE GREAT WAR 1914 - 18
WITH THE IMPERIAL CAMEL CORPS IN THE GREAT WAR by Geoffrey Inchbald

The story of a serving officer with the British 2nd battalion against the Senussi and during the Palestine campaign.

SOFTCOVER : **ISBN 1-84677-007-6**
HARDCOVER : **ISBN 1-84677-012-2**

EW3 EYEWITNESS TO WAR SERIES
THE KHAKEE RESSALAH
by Robert Henry Wallace Dunlop

Service & adventure with the Meerut Volunteer Horse During the Indian Mutiny 1857-1858.

SOFTCOVER : **ISBN 1-84677-009-2**
HARDCOVER : **ISBN 1-84677-017-3**

WF1 THE WARFARE FICTION SERIES
NAPOLEONIC WAR STORIES
by Sir Arthur Quiller-Couch

Tales of soldiers, spies, battles & Sieges from the Peninsular & Waterloo campaigns

SOFTCOVER : **ISBN 1-84677-003-3**
HARDCOVER : **ISBN 1-84677-014-9**

AVAILABLE ONLINE AT
www.leonaur.com
AND OTHER GOOD BOOK STORES

LEONAUR

ALSO FROM LEONAUR

AVAILABLE IN SOFTCOVER OR HARDCOVER WITH DUST JACKET

EW2 EYEWITNESS TO WAR SERIES
CAPTAIN OF THE 95th (Rifles) by Jonathan Leach

An officer of Wellington's Sharpshooters during the
Peninsular, South of France and Waterloo Campaigns
of the Napoleonic Wars.

SOFTCOVER : **ISBN 1-84677-001-7**
HARDCOVER : **ISBN 1-84677-016-5**

WFI THE WARFARE FICTION SERIES
NAPOLEONIC WAR STORIES
by Sir Arthur Quiller-Couch

Tales of soldiers, spies, battles & Sieges from the
Peninsular & Waterloo campaigns

SOFTCOVER : **ISBN 1-84677-003-3**
HARDCOVER : **ISBN 1-84677-014-9**

EWI EYEWITNESS TO WAR SERIES
RIFLEMAN COSTELLO by Edward Costello

The adventures of a soldier of the 95th (Rifles) in the Peninsular
& Waterloo Campaigns of the Napoleonic wars.

SOFTCOVER : **ISBN 1-84677-000-9**
HARDCOVER : **ISBN 1-84677-018-1**

MCI THE MILITARY COMMANDERS SERIES
**JOURNALS OF ROBERT ROGERS OF THE
RANGERS** by Robert Rogers

The exploits of Rogers & the Rangers in his own words
during 1755-1761 in the French & Indian War.

SOFTCOVER : **ISBN 1-84677-002-5**
HARDCOVER : **ISBN 1-84677-010-6**

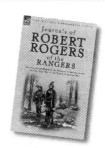

AVAILABLE ONLINE AT
www.leonaur.com
AND OTHER GOOD BOOK STORES

CPSIA information can be obtained at www.ICGtesting.com
Printed in the USA
BVOW07s1552161213

339281BV00001B/121/A

9 781846 770227